What R

Emily's work allows the ri ... to bring depth to the biblical truths we confess in the Apostles' Creed. Her mission stories help us see the wonder of our Lord's incomprehensible love for all people. We grow to understand that God's Word speaks to every language and culture and are reminded of how we have allowed our own culture to raise barriers to a right relationship with God. This work, which is for Christians and non-Christians, illustrates that confession is also proclamation.

REV. DR. JOHN MEHL, EXECUTIVE DIRECTOR OF MISSION OF CHRIST NETWORK

In a world of dramatic cultural changes, the story of God's love for His people is even more comforting. Emily Belvery's study of the Apostles' Creed connects participants to the historic, universal truths narrated by the Creed and the deep insights brought by a multi-cultural discussion of the faith. Her extensive notes and references for leaders make this study simple to use for any group. Her personal stories of mission and ministry in East Asia reveal how cross-cultural discussions of the biblical faith will deepen and broaden our perspectives on the creedal faith.

REV. JOEL SCHEIWE, SENIOR PASTOR, CHURCH OF ALL NATIONS, HONG KONG

I believe you will find this book refreshing and renewing. I did. You are invited beyond superficiality into the richness of the Apostles' Creed and the lively and comforting confession found there. But there is more! Emily Belvery equips the reader to share the true God with others (Evangelism! Mission!) in a relatable and practical way based on the Creed. Inspiring stories from her work in Asian countries brings biblical theology to a very useful level for everyday relationships inside and especially outside the community of believers. Church professionals and laity alike will find the book insightful, faithful, and helpful as they teach, equip, and lead for the sake of Christ's Church and mission! In a world of disconnection, this book connects to great things and great opportunities.

REV. DR. ALLAN BUSS, PRESIDENT, NORTHERN ILLINOIS DISTRICT LCMS

The fundamental truths of our shared Christian faith are the heartbeat of this refreshing Bible study. Author Emily Belvery brings fresh insight to this amazing ancient Creed that crosses cultures, languages, and nations. She then delves more deeply into the tenets of our triune faith, unpacking each petition through thoughtful Scripture study, engaging essays, compelling questions, and discussion topics. Both articulate and conversational, this unique study has made my profession of the Apostles' Creed all the richer and renewed my fervor to live out the faith that I confess together with all believers.

DEB BURMA, CHRISTIAN SPEAKER AND AUTHOR OF *JOY: A STUDY OF PHILIPPIANS*, *BE STILL AND KNOW*, AND *LIVING A CHOCOLATE LIFE*

Emily Belvery has produced a Scripture-rich study of the Apostles' Creed. Both new and reviewing Christians will welcome it as a tool to nurture their faith and life in Christ, increasing their zeal to share the Gospel with others. Participants will especially value the essays at the end of each chapter. These essays reveal how the Holy Spirit used Emily as a missionary in Taiwan to speak apostolic truth substantively, humbly, and compassionately, reaching across cultural and religious canyons. Upon reading the last essay, your response will likely be similar to mine: "Sister Emily, teach me more!"

REV. CHARLES BLANCO, PROFESSOR OF THEOLOGY, CONCORDIA UNIVERSITY NEBRASKA

TOGETHER WE BELIEVE

A Study of the Apostles' Creed

Emily Belvery

CONCORDIA PUBLISHING HOUSE • SAINT LOUIS

DEDICATION

To Asian brothers and sisters,
who taught me so much about walking with Jesus,
and
to Jacob and Nora, who make every place
that we're together home.

Published by Concordia Publishing House
3558 S. Jefferson Ave., St. Louis, MO 63118-3968
1-800-325-3040 • cph.org

◊ 1 2 3 4 5 6 7 8 9 10   31 30 29 28 27 26 25 24 23 22

ACKNOWLEDGMENTS

■ ■ ■

Thank you to the colleagues, students, teachers, and friends in Asia who mentored me, prayed with and for me, put up with my language and cultural blunders, and studied the Scriptures with me.

There are few things as exciting or spiritually energizing as teaching, praying, and conversing with new Christians. Thank you to the church Bible study students who first studied these lessons with me and brought their questions and insights to the themes and passages. "I am sure of this, that He who began a good work in you will bring it to completion at the day of Jesus Christ" (Philippians 1:6).

An emphasis on education is one of the great gifts of a Lutheran heritage, and so much of what is contained in these chapters comes from the wisdom of my own teachers. Thank you to a lifetime of Bible teachers—from parents and grandparents to pastors and Sunday School teachers to professors at Concordia University Nebraska—who faithfully taught me the Scriptures and answered oh so many questions.

While being far from my family was unquestioningly the hardest thing about living overseas, the spiritual and emotional support of my family is also what made it possible for me to go. Thank you to my parents, Jonathan and Ruth Barz, and siblings, Megan and Zachary, for the years of faith formation that came from growing up in a Christ-centered home and for ongoing and unconditional love and support.

Thank you to my beloved husband, Jacob, who loved me enough to follow me to Asia; who prays with and for me in groans or words; and who is always ready to offer feedback, advice, and a steady vote of confidence. And thank you to my sweet baby, Nora, who made me a mother and has given me a glimpse of the instant, unconditional love the Father has for His children.

Most of all, all thanks and praise be to God our Father and Creator, Christ our Redeemer and King, and the Spirit who creates and nurtures faith.

CONTENTS

■ ■ ■

The Apostles' Creed

I believe in God, the Father Almighty,

    maker of heaven and earth.

And in Jesus Christ, His only Son, our Lord,

    who was conceived by the Holy Spirit,

    born of the virgin Mary,

    suffered under Pontius Pilate,

    was crucified, died and was buried.

    He descended into hell.

    The third day He rose again from the dead.

    He ascended into heaven

    and sits at the right hand of God the Father Almighty.

    From thence He will come to judge the living and the dead.

I believe in the Holy Spirit,

    the holy Christian Church,

     the communion of saints,

    the forgiveness of sins,

    the resurrection of the body,

    and the life ☩ everlasting. Amen.

PREFACE

I was excited but clueless when I arrived on the island of Taiwan as a twenty-one-year-old missionary teacher, outfitted with a brand-new diploma, lots of ideas about teaching (some better than others), and a desire to make a difference. Although I taught middle school classes in English, Mandarin language study was a priority for me for engaging in daily life, ministry, and relationship building. One of the first things I was determined to learn in Mandarin was how to recite the Apostles' Creed. It certainly was mere recitation. Given that I was learning phrases like "I am American" and "Where is the bathroom?" in my language classes, the Mandarin for "conceived by the Holy Spirit" was well, well beyond my language level. Yet week by week, a fellow American teacher and I met with Taiwanese Christian sisters from our church to work our way through this ancient Creed, Chinese character by Chinese character, phrase by phrase.

Few of the vocabulary words I learned in order to recite the Creed helped me in daily conversation. *Almighty* and *crucified* didn't come up much in trips to the grocery store or when ordering rice or noodles for dinner, so such theological language study could have been seen as premature and impractical. Yet learning the Creed was a priority for me, first because my ultimate goal in language study was to be able to speak the Gospel in people's heart language (native language), and second because I found great joy in being able to confess these words together with Taiwanese Christians each Sunday. This unity of faith and professing of specific words and ideas to express this faith—a single confession handed down across time and shared across borders and cultures and languages—was a powerful comfort in a period when my life had been turned upside down. I felt like an outsider in every aspect of daily life and frequently heard *waiguoren*, the Mandarin word for "foreigner," slung in my direction (usually combined with a pointed finger). But when I sat in the pews of Salvation Lutheran Church behind my Mandarin teachers, confessing together our faith in the triune God, I was no longer a stranger or alien but a fellow citizen of the Kingdom and a sister in the household of God (Ephesians 2:19).

Years later when I had the opportunity to write and teach this study of the Apostles' Creed to young Christians in a different large Asian city, I realized afresh the power and importance of this confession of faith. My students, most of them new to the Christian faith, found in the Creed not only unity with other believers but also a critical foundation of faith and doctrine. When every page of Scripture was new to them and they were unsure where to begin, the Creed offered a framework into which they could fit each passage they encountered. Not only that, but as we studied together, these Asian brothers and sisters also brought to the truths of Scripture questions, perceptions, and insights I hadn't considered.

When I told a Dutch classmate (at the Chinese language center where I later studied) that I had come to new understandings of Christianity by serving in Taiwan, he was confused. He wondered what Asians could teach me about this Western religion, a foreign Christian culture that we missionaries were "imposing" upon Taiwanese. For we who believe in Christ, though, such reciprocal learning shouldn't be a surprise. God, the author of creation and Lord of a heavenly city that will one day be filled with "the glory and the honor of the nations," has not restricted

His work or His presence to one culture or language (Revelation 21:26). God, who "made from one man every nation of mankind to live on all the face of the earth . . . that they should seek God, and perhaps feel their way toward Him and find Him," is seeking after and working among every nation of people. God is "not far from each one of us"; He has called all people His offspring (Acts 17:26–27).

And so, my aim in this study is twofold. The first is to return to the most basic truths of the Christian faith in a way that is accessible to new Christians and to those returning to the faith (a demographic many of our churches too often fail to expect or address in Bible study) and to also draw lifelong believers deeper into these familiar truths and out into the daily life applications of these beliefs. The second aim is to invite North American Christians into conversation with our Asian brothers and sisters. Using questions and stories shaped by missionary experiences, I hope to help believers remember again the awesome beauty of the Gospel and unique nature of our God, and to think in new and fresh ways about what these truths mean for our lives.

STUDY OVERVIEW

■ ■ ■

Whether you are a new Christian or a lifelong believer, this study is designed to lead you in an in-depth and practical study of the Apostles' Creed. While the words are deeply familiar to most believers, the meaning and implications of this ancient statement of faith may not be something you consider often or may be something you haven't studied since confirmation. Each lesson leads participants through relevant Bible passages to draw out the meaning of the article of the Creed being considered. The application questions and discussion topics that follow are meant to help you make connections between faith and life and to give you tools to share your faith when you encounter the questions of others.

Study Format

While the leader is provided with additional notes and will take responsibility for preparing for and directing the study time and discussion, the bulk of the learning will come from all participants reading and responding to the biblical texts directly and from engaging in group conversation. Interacting with the text and applying it to your own life will help make this learning lasting and transformative. All believers are invited to "read, mark, learn, and inwardly digest"[1] the words of Scripture, and what better place to practice and learn these skills than in study with other Christians?

Student pages are workbook-like and provide space for writing directly in this book. Use this space to take notes on your own answers as well as the comments of others, and feel free to highlight and otherwise mark up this book to make it a unique and personal discovery of the Creed.

For each session, it will be important to bring a study Bible and something to write with. Feel free to write in your Bible, highlight, and underline passages and notes that inform your study. God, in His Word, speaks to you personally and intends for you to take it to heart. Looking back later on passages you have highlighted and on notes added from further Bible study can serve as a beautiful record of God's ongoing work to guide you into deeper knowledge of Him.

Lesson Format

Each lesson includes the following:

- **Introduction questions** to help you get to know other participants

- **Opening discussion** questions to help you begin to think about the key themes of the lesson and their meaning for our lives

- **Bible readings** paired with general **questions** about the text, **Digging Deeper** questions to challenge and stimulate thinking, and **Application** questions that connect the text to everyday thoughts and actions

- Ideas for **prayer time**

- A supplemental **hymn,** which can be read or prayed aloud, listened to, or sung together, as the setting allows

- A **topical essay** that draws on the author's mission experiences

INTRODUCTION TO THE CREED

■ ■ ■

What Is the Apostles' Creed?

Drawn from the Scriptures, the Apostles' Creed is a statement of what Christians believe. As Luther explains, it "sets forth to us everything that we must expect and receive from God. To state it quite briefly, the Creed teaches us to know Him fully [Ephesians 3:19]."[2] It was not written by the apostles themselves, but it confesses the teaching of the apostles as written by them in the Bible. It is one of three creeds used in the Christian Church, including also the Nicene and the Athanasian Creeds, and it is the most concise and most commonly used, as well as being the Creed used in Luther's Catechisms.

The Apostles' Creed is divided into three articles, with each article focused on one person of the Trinity. The First Article tells us about the Father and our creation. Here we begin to answer the question of who this God is that we are to "fear, love, and trust in . . . above all things."[3] The Second Article, the longest of the three, describes Christ and our redemption. "The entire Gospel that we preach is based on this point, that we properly understand this article as that upon which our salvation and all our happiness rests. It is so rich and complete that we can never learn it fully."[4] The Third Article focuses upon the Holy Spirit and our sanctification (how He makes us holy). This sanctification is an ongoing work, "for now we are only half pure and holy. So the Holy Spirit always has some reason to continue His work in us through the Word. He must daily administer forgiveness until we reach the life to come."[5]

For more explanation of the Creed as understood in Lutheran theology, see Luther's Small and Large Catechisms.

When Do We Use the Apostles' Creed?

The Apostles' Creed is used in corporate worship, often following the sermon as a response to the message and a communal professing of our faith. While we speak the Lord's Prayer collectively with heads bowed in prayer to God, we can speak the Creed together with heads raised and eyes upon one another, confessing to one another and to the world who we know the triune God to be.

The Apostles' Creed is also used in the Baptism liturgy, where candidates (or their sponsors) confess, using the words of the Creed, what they believe about the triune God into whose name we are baptized. Similarly, the words of the Apostles' Creed are used in the confirmation liturgy to explain the faith we are confirming. (Typically, the Nicene Creed is used with Communion services.) Many responsive-prayer and evening and morning prayer services also include the Apostles' Creed, including the funeral liturgy, where the pastor invites the congregation to profess the Creed as a confession of our baptismal faith and hope for everlasting life.

The Creed may also be used in the traditional order of daily prayer for individual and family devotion time. This simple and brief form of prayer includes the Lord's Prayer, Scripture and psalm readings, and a hymn, along with prayers for ourselves and for others.

Why Study the Apostles' Creed?

To be perhaps overly simplistic, the Apostles' Creed is worth studying because we use it often and so should be familiar with it. Many Lutherans will have studied the Creed from Luther's Small Catechism as part of their confirmation instruction, but they may be many years removed from this instruction and not remember it well. Other Christians who grew up in nonliturgical churches may never have studied the Creed or used it only sporadically.

When I first taught this study in the mission field, I had an American student who commented that she had never used the Apostles' Creed in her home congregation. She was surprised and even skeptical about using it as a study topic, assuming it to be ancient, rote, and unhelpful. However, as we began studying together, she was pleasantly surprised by how well it summed up the Christian faith and how useful it was both for the new Christians in our class trying to make sense of the Scriptures and for her as she sought to clearly share her faith with others.

The Creed gives us a foundation on which to build our understanding of the Scriptures and a guide that can aid us in navigating challenging passages or theological questions. For new Christians or those newly returning to the faith, it offers a starting place to understand the basic tenets of our faith and a framework into which they can fit all newly acquired theological understanding. For mature Christians, the Creed is an outline of the basic teachings of Christianity, which can be helpful in seeking to clearly articulate to others what it is we believe. And for all believers, the Creed is a helpful litmus test for determining which religious bodies are Christian denominations and which are unchristian cults or heresies.

Wherever you are in your faith life, may this study of the Apostles' Creed further your understanding of our triune God and deepen your faith in Jesus' forgiveness, mercy, and salvation. To God be the glory!

Participant Pages

ARTICLE 1:
WHAT IS GOD LIKE?

■ ■ ■

"I believe in God, the Father Almighty,
Maker of heaven and earth."

▪▪ CATECHISM REFERENCE

What does this mean? I believe that God has made me and all creatures; that He has given me my body and soul, eyes, ears, and all my members, my reason and all my senses, and still takes care of them. He also gives me clothing and shoes, food and drink, house and home, wife and children, land, animals, and all I have. He richly and daily provides me with all that I need to support this body and life. He defends me against all danger and guards and protects me from all evil. All this He does only out of fatherly, divine goodness and mercy, without any merit or worthiness in me. For all this it is my duty to thank and praise, serve and obey Him.

This is most certainly true.[6]

▪▪ OPENING PRAYER

▪▪ INTRODUCTION QUESTION

Choose one of the following questions to answer:

1. What does your name mean?
2. How did your parents pick your name?
3. What other names or nicknames do people call you?

▪▪ OPENING DISCUSSION

God is almighty (has all power) and He loves you as a father. What would it mean for us if God were only powerful but not loving?

....

....

....

....

....

What would it mean for us if God were only loving but not powerful?

....

....

....

....

....

▪▪ I. GOD IS THE MAKER OF HEAVEN AND EARTH.

Read **Acts 17:24–29.**

    A. Where did everything in the world come from?

....

....

....

....

....

    B. In what ways is God still working in creation and our lives? On a scale from 1 to 10, how involved is He in the events of daily life?

....

....

....

....

....

    C. What is God's purpose for creating us and working in our lives?

....

....

....

....

....

DIGGING DEEPER

Reread **Acts 17:25**.

1. Does God need you to do things for Him? What, then, does it mean to serve Him?

....

....

....

....

....

2. Who does need your help? Why do we help others?

....

....

....

....

....

APPLICATION

God made everything. If you believe this fact, it changes how you view all of life! Below are six situations you might encounter in conversations with others.[7] How would you answer in each situation based on what we've read in Acts 17 or by referencing other Bible passages about God as our Creator?

1. If someone says, "I do not have much value"?

2. If someone says, "My life has no meaning"?

3. If someone is considering aborting an unborn child?

4. If someone doesn't care what effect his or her actions have on the environment?

5. If someone says, "I can do anything I want to. Nobody has the right to tell me what is right or wrong"?

6. If someone says, "All gods are the same"?

▪️ II. GOD IS OUR FATHER.

Read **Luke 15:11–24**.

A. What things did the younger son do to his father? How do you imagine the father felt?

....

....

....

....

....

B. How did the father show unconditional love for the son? What is astonishing about the father's actions?

....

....

....

....

....

C. How are we like the younger son? How is God like the father?

....

....

....

....

....

APPLICATION

In what ways can you see yourself in the older son? How was his view of the father also distorted? Are there some of God's children (our lost siblings!) that He's more eager to welcome back into the family than we are?

....

....

....

....

....

DIGGING DEEPER

Forgiveness is not free. What did it cost the father to forgive his son? What do you think the father might have suffered for him? What does it cost us to forgive others? What did it cost Jesus to forgive us?

....

....

....

....

APPLICATION

If God is *our* Father, how does that change how we relate to one another?

....

....

....

....

....

▪▪ PRAYER PROMPT

Father God, show us our sin. Reveal the things we have thought, said, and done that are not pleasing to You. Forgive us for our disloyalty and the pain we've caused You, but also for our unforgiveness and unwillingness to welcome back lost siblings.

(Take time for silent confession.)

PRAY TOGETHER

"Have mercy on me, O God, according to Your steadfast love; according to Your abundant mercy blot out my transgressions. . . . Purge me with hyssop, and I shall be clean; wash me, and I shall be whiter than snow. . . . Create in me a clean heart, O God, and renew a right spirit within me. . . . Restore to me the joy of Your salvation, and uphold me with a willing spirit." (PSALM 51:1, 7, 10, 12)

■ HYMN

Lord of All Nations, Grant Me Grace

Lord of all nations, grant me grace
To love all people, ev'ry race;
And in each person may I see
My kindred, loved, redeemed by Thee.

Break down the wall that would divide
Thy children, Lord, on ev'ry side.
My neighbor's good let me pursue;
Let Christian love bind warm and true.

Forgive me, Lord, where I have erred
By loveless act and thoughtless word.
Make me to see the wrong I do
Will grieve my wounded Lord anew.

Give me Thy courage, Lord, to speak
Whenever strong oppress the weak.
Should I myself the victim be,
Help me forgive, rememb'ring Thee.

With Thine own love may I be filled
And by Thy Holy Spirit willed,
That all I touch, where're I be,
May be divinely touched by Thee. (*LSB* 844)

Reading the Prodigal Son in Asia

On the whole, ethnic Chinese are less direct and less confrontational than Americans, yet somehow I ended up with two very blunt Chinese tutors. My Taiwanese Mandarin tutor began my first lesson by teaching me the phrase "Don't be afraid" and then quickly followed this by teaching me to understand the words "Wrong. Say it again." My other tutor, a young atheist woman, told me after we read the story of the prodigal son together, "This is a stupid story. I always thought Jesus was probably a wise teacher, but now I'm not convinced He was." She railed about how unfair the whole story was and how ridiculous the actions of the father seemed. She immediately identified with the older son—after all she was a good, filial, loyal daughter to her parents—and was horrified at the injustice the son suffered. How could he be expected to not only welcome back his delinquent brother but also embrace him and give to him new riches out of his own half of the inheritance? (After all, the older son's half was all the family had left.) How could God be so unjust?

Eventually, as a concessionary attempt to understand the story, she concluded, "Well, maybe American parents would be like this, but an Asian father would never do this. He would never openly welcome back the son, and he certainly wouldn't give him a place of honor in the family again. What if the son takes the new gifts from the father and runs off again on another spending spree? I guess this story just makes more sense to Westerners."

More likely, however, it is we Westerners who have forgotten the scandal of the parables, and my tutor who reacted more like Jesus' Jewish audience would have. I was told once that the key to understanding the parables is to find the action that makes no human sense and then recognize this as God's action in the story. In collective cultures (cultures that focus on the needs and priorities of the group rather than the individual—a category that involves a majority of world cultures), a child's life is not his own, and not even after the parents' deaths is his inheritance his own. In Chinese, names begin with the surname, the family name being the primary marker of identity. No major decisions are made without family input; parents help shape children's thoughts about career, marriage, parenting, and so forth. Just as parents care for children in their youth, so children care for parents in their old age, and many young Chinese adults send money to their parents monthly. In this culture, then, the parable is difficult, much as it was challenging to Jesus' Jewish audience and probably should be to us too. The inheritance the younger son squandered was not just a waste of his own possessions; it was also the loss of money that was to provide for extended family, servants, and estate. This is not just a story about a son who made poor life decisions but also one about a son who dragged down with him into shame and disgrace his father and all the household.

When I taught middle school in Taiwan, I once asked my students to write about a family memory. One student wrote about having had to confess to his parents—on the same day as his birthday—that he had scored poorly on major exams. Although in shame he ran away from home, his mother met up with him to talk. He wrote:

> My mom asked me to go to 7-11 with her, and she told me that they were really upset. We sat at the table in 7-11 together, face-to-face. She told me that if I really didn't want to be her son, I could choose to not be, and she told me that they had prepared a cake for me, but since they knew that I ran away, they returned it. She asked me to give her back the

gift she had given me. She said I was evil, and they didn't want to talk to me.

When I got home with my mom, she said nothing and went upstairs. For the whole night, I couldn't sleep well; I felt really guilty. For the next couple of days, my parents didn't talk to me and pretended they didn't see me or hear me.

While this story may seem horrifyingly extreme to many of us, the reality is that in a collective culture like Taiwan's—a place with high emphasis on academics and pressure to perform—my student's parents had only two choices. They could admit that they had a son who wasn't very good at school and take onto themselves the shame that came with this admission. His failure was their failure. His future success (or lack thereof) defined the family's reputation. Or—as they chose in this instance—they could push him away and preserve their own honor. He could choose to not be their son and free them from bearing his failure.

This is the choice, too, of the father in Jesus' parable. This is the choice of God: to bear the shame our sin deserves or to push us away and maintain His own honor. On the cross, Christ bore the disgrace brought upon God's name and His family by every one of us disloyal children. He identified with our evil, even though we, in our sinful rebellion, chose to not be identified as children of God. But by the resurrection, God restored His own honor and offered eternal honor and a secure place in the family to every redeemed son and daughter. God, who said at Christ's Baptism, "This is My beloved Son, with whom I am well pleased" (Matthew 3:17), says to us who are baptized into Christ, "You are My beloved child. I am well pleased with you."

As my tutor and I unpacked the parable further, I told her that this unfair love of God is exactly what makes it possible for us to love people in our lives. My tutor described how she constantly kept mental score of what her husband had done for her and what she owed him back. Their marriage was not strained or acrimonious from her perspective. She just didn't want to end up giving more than she got; she wanted things to be fair. This is the logic of the world, but it is not the way of a life of grace. We who know the boundless love of the Father have a surplus of honor and grace to share with others in our lives without worrying if they will pay us back.

While we can each identify at times with the older son, we must admit we have also been the younger son. Each of us has failed to live as a child of God in the world, has dishonored His name among others, and has selfishly squandered the gifts He has given us—gifts that should be used to glorify the Father and to care for others. However, our prodigal (recklessly extravagant!) God is unfair with us. He does not "deal with us according to our sins nor repay us according to our iniquities" (Psalm 103:10) but welcomes us back with open arms and rich gifts—scandalously lavishing heavenly wealth on sinful children who could (and too often do!) wander from His side and waste His gifts once more. But because we know and have experienced this unfair love of the Father, we are freed to live with true love in our earthly relationships. We don't have to keep score, don't have to worry about what is owed back to us, don't need to fear investing more in a relationship than the other person will give in return. We are free to love with prodigal abandon because we have a sure and abiding home in the love of the Father.

ARTICLE 2:
NAMES AND TITLES OF JESUS

■ ■ ■

". . . And in Jesus Christ, His
only Son, our Lord . . ."

▋▋ CATECHISM REFERENCE

You shall not misuse the name of the LORD your God.

*W*hat does this mean? We should fear and love God so that we do not curse, swear, use satanic arts, lie, or deceive by His name, but call upon it in every trouble, pray, praise, and give thanks.[8]

█▪ OPENING PRAYER

█▪ INTRODUCTION QUESTION

Pick one name of Jesus you find interesting, comforting, or hard to understand. Explain to your group why you picked it.

This phrase from the Creed gives us four names or titles: Jesus is the Christ, the Son, and our Lord. Scripture gives us many, many names, titles, and offices of Jesus! In a small group, look at one of the names or titles and the Bible references in the list that follows, and answer the questions. Then share your findings with the full group.

Example: *Jesus—Matthew 1:18–21* (Do this one together as a class.)

1. What does this name/title mean?

....

2. What does this name/title say about who Jesus is?

....

3. What does this name/title say about what Jesus did/does?

....

4. When might you want to pray using this name/title?

....

5. Draw a picture or think of an image to represent this name/title.

....

█▪ NAMES AND TITLES OF JESUS

A. Immanuel—Matthew 1:18–23; John 14:9–11

1. What does this name/title mean?

....

2. What does this name/title say about who Jesus is?

....

3. What does this name/title say about what Jesus did/does?

....

4. When might you want to pray using this name/title?

....

5. Draw a picture or think of an image to represent this name/title.

....

B. Christ/Messiah—John 1:40–42; John 4:25–26; John 20:30–31 (See Note A on page 46.)

1. What does this name/title mean?

....

2. What does this name/title say about who Jesus is?

....

3. What does this name/title say about what Jesus did/does?

....

4. When might you want to pray using this name/title?

....

5. Draw a picture or think of an image to represent this name/title.

....

C. The Word—John 1:1–3, 14 (read the verses again, substituting "Jesus" every time you see "Word" or "He"); Psalm 33:6

1. What does this name/title mean?

....

2. What does this name/title say about who Jesus is?

....

3. What does this name/title say about what Jesus did/does?

....

4. When might you want to pray using this name/title?

....

5. Draw a picture or think of an image to represent this name/title.

....

D. Son of God—Mark 1:1, 9–11; John 5:17–23
(Does this mean Jesus is not God?)

1. What does this name/title mean?

....

2. What does this name/title say about who Jesus is?

....

3. What does this name/title say about what Jesus did/does?

....

4. When might you want to pray using this name/title?

....

5. Draw a picture or think of an image to represent this name/title.

....

E. Son of Man—Daniel 7:13–14; Mark 10:43–45; Matthew 26:63–65 (See Note B on page 46.)

1. What does this name/title mean?

....

2. What does this name/title say about who Jesus is?

....

3. What does this name/title say about what Jesus did/does?

....

4. When might you want to pray using this name/title?

....

5. Draw a picture or think of an image to represent this name/title.

....

F. Lord—Romans 10:9–13; Philippians 2:9–11

1. What does this name/title mean?

....

2. What does this name/title say about who Jesus is?

....

3. What does this name/title say about what Jesus did/does?

....

4. When might you want to pray using this name/title?

....

5. Draw a picture or think of an image to represent this name/title.

....

G. Lamb of God—John 1:29–31; Hebrews 10:1–10

1. What does this name/title mean?

....

2. What does this name/title say about who Jesus is?

....

3. What does this name/title say about what Jesus did/does?

....

4. When might you want to pray using this name/title?

....

5. Draw a picture or think of an image to represent this name/title.

....

H. Light of the World—John 8:12; Matthew 4:12–17

1. What does this name/title mean?

....

2. What does this name/title say about who Jesus is?

....

3. What does this name/title say about what Jesus did/does?

....

4. When might you want to pray using this name/title?

....

5. Draw a picture or think of an image to represent this name/title.

....

I. The Resurrection and the Life—John 11:23–27; 1 Corinthians 15:20–23

1. What does this name/title mean?

....

2. What does this name/title say about who Jesus is?

....

3. What does this name/title say about what Jesus did/does?

....

4. When might you want to pray using this name/title?

....

5. Draw a picture or think of an image to represent this name/title.

....

J. Prophet—Deuteronomy 18:15–19; Acts 3:19–23; Luke 7:14–16; Matthew 24:3–14 (See Note C on page 46.)

1. What does this name/title mean?

....

2. What does this name/title say about who Jesus is?

....

3. What does this name/title say about what Jesus did/does?

....

4. When might you want to pray using this name/title?

....

5. Draw a picture or think of an image to represent this name/title.

....

K. Priest—Hebrews 7:23–27; Hebrews 4:14–16

1. What does this name/title mean?

....

2. What does this name/title say about who Jesus is?

....

3. What does this name/title say about what Jesus did/does?

....

4. When might you want to pray using this name/title?

....

5. Draw a picture or think of an image to represent this name/title.

....

L. King/King of kings—Revelation 1:4–5; John 18:33–37

1. What does this name/title mean?

....

2. What does this name/title say about who Jesus is?

....

3. What does this name/title say about what Jesus did/does?

....

4. When might you want to pray using this name/title?

....

5. Draw a picture or think of an image to represent this name/title.

....

▟▛ NOTES AND EXPLANATIONS

NOTE A

Christ is Greek and *Messiah* is Hebrew, but they both have the same meaning: "anointed one." This was the title the Jews used for the promised Savior, the special, chosen leader that God would send to save both the Jews and the whole world.

NOTE B

"Son of Man" (Jesus' most common way of referencing Himself) carries a double meaning. It is a way of emphasizing His humanity, contrasting with the title Son of God. However, this name is also a powerful Old Testament reference to Daniel 7. Jesus claimed to be the "one like a son of man" (Daniel 7:13), holy and worthy of worship, whom Daniel saw in heaven. This claim is what so greatly upset the high priest.

NOTE C

Prophets in the Old Testament had three jobs:

1. Speak God's words to people
2. Prophesy
3. Perform healings and miracles

Putting it all together, what have we learned about who Jesus is and what He did then and does for us now? Take notes as others share their findings.

WHO JESUS IS	WHAT JESUS DID/DOES

So that at the name of Jesus every knee should bow, in heaven and on earth and under the earth.

(PHILIPPIANS 2:10)

PRAYER PROMPTS

- *Thank God for sending Jesus, and praise Jesus for who He is.*
- *Pray for grace to know Jesus more.*
- *Pray requests based on the name of Jesus that you studied.*

HYMN

How Sweet the Name of Jesus Sounds

How sweet the name of Jesus sounds,
In a believer's ear!
It soothes our sorrows, heals our wounds,
And drives away our fear.

It makes the wounded spirit whole,
And calms the heart's unrest;
'Tis manna to the hungry soul
And to the weary, rest.

Dear name! The rock on which I build,
My shield and hiding place;
My never-failing treasury filled,
With boundless stores of grace.

O Jesus, shepherd, guardian friend,
My Prophet, Priest, and King.
My Lord, my life, my way, my end,
Accept the praise I bring.

How weak the effort of my heart,
How cold my warmest thought!
But when I see Thee as Thou art,
I'll praise Thee as I ought.

Till then I would Thy love proclaim
With ev'ry fleeting breath;
And may the music of Thy name
Refresh my soul in death!

Prayer: Foreign or Familiar?

When I talked with students in Taiwan about the idea of Christian prayer, they found the topic at once familiar and strange. Most Taiwanese practice a combination of Buddhism and Daoism with ancestor worship mixed in, a blend of spiritual practices that is not as much theological or doctrinal as it is intensely practical in focus. As my colleague, friend, and mentor Barb Rebentisch explained to me, Taiwanese gods are much like doctors. Each specializes in an aspect of human life, so when people are facing a problem (infertility, job loss, impending exams, etc.), they go to one temple to see the relevant "specialist" (idol), pay the bill (often cash or perhaps an offering of fruit or the burning of incense), and then ask this god to fix the problem. If after worshiping and making the request a person is still childless or doesn't receive a promotion, he or she then seeks out a different temple and a different god and hopes that this one can solve the problem.

Thus, when we talked about prayer in class, at first glance it was familiar to my students. There was nothing strange sounding about appealing to a spiritual power for aid, and if they themselves had unsolved problems, why not add another god to the list of powers they appealed to? Many students were willing to share prayer requests when I asked at the beginning of class (especially around exam time!), and they were curious to know if they, too, could pray to the Christian God. As they saw it, there was certainly no harm and possibly great benefit. But the more we talked about Christian prayer and who it is we pray to, the more it became clear that what we mean by prayer is something very different indeed.

Christian prayer is talking with the Father, a relational endeavor. We have an open invitation to approach the Father in prayer because of Christ's sacrifice, and God promises to hear and answer. Prayer certainly involves needs and requests, but this is not its sole purpose. If I called my dad only when I wanted money, we would have a terrible relationship; yet if I had real need and didn't go to my dad for help, he would also be hurt that I had kept this struggle from him and denied him the opportunity to help. I warned my students that asking for something in prayer didn't mean they would receive it, just as a good father doesn't say yes to everything a child requests. Our God is not an idol with whom we can barter. If God owed us answered prayer in response to our devotion, He would be below us in status, an inferior for us to command rather than a Lord for us to obey. And yet God delights in listening to us and in answering our prayers to Him.

When we pray, we know that God may answer in any number of ways according to His perfect knowledge and will. While at first not being guaranteed whatever they prayed for sounded like bad news to my students, this truth is what makes Christian prayer possible. How terrifying it would be to pray if we knew God would *always* give us what we asked! How could we know if our prayer was asking for the right thing, at the right time, and in the right way? Much as in fairy tales where characters foolishly ask for wishes that end up causing more harm than good, might our prayers not also accidentally call down curses rather than blessings upon ourselves and others?

As a further point of contrast with Taiwanese traditional religion, we as Christians have beautiful freedom to pray at all times and in all circumstances. Taiwanese idol worship requires visiting specific temples to offer prayers, asking yes-or-no questions to be answered with divination blocks, or asking more-complex questions to be answered through a priest's interpretation of lines of ancient poetry. The location and the topic of the prayer is limited. Using the previous analogy, when I visit my doctor, he is on a tight schedule and has time to address only the health problem for which I am seeking his help. He doesn't want to hear about my life, my relationships, my hopes and dreams. But my earthly father does. And so does our heavenly Father! Christian prayer, then, is a refuge in all times, an opportunity to sit in the throne room of God and "pour out your heart like water before the presence of the Lord" (Lamentations 2:19).

And the true beauty of Christian prayer—as each of these names and titles of Jesus further elucidates—lies in who we are praying to. We pray to Immanuel, Christ who is ever present with us. We pray to the anointed and long-awaited Christ. We pray to the Holy Son of God, who is at once an understanding and exalted Son of Man. We pray to the creating and sustaining Word of God, the Light that shatters darkness, the Resurrection that forever conquered death and the grave.

Immanuel was a name of God that took on even more poignant meaning for me when I moved across the ocean where everyone I knew and loved was thirteen time zones away. I felt as if I had stepped into another world, yet I knew that "if I take the wings of the morning and dwell in the uttermost parts of the sea, even there Your hand shall lead me, and Your right hand shall hold me" (Psalm 139:9–10). Immanuel is a name of God that Chinese Christians hold dear and use often, a promise of Christ's presence that they have seen marvelously fulfilled across a challenging Church history of threat and persecution. Immanuel is the promise that God is with us wherever we are, not bound by place or limited in presence.

This promise of omnipresence might be something we take for granted, but it is marvelously beyond expectation for many. Taiwanese gods are tied to specific places, idols placed in fields or kitchens or carried with a person to offer blessing and protection. Temples are the place to go to offer supplication because that is where the gods are believed to be present to answer. I once told a Mongolian friend that I often prayed while riding my bicycle around our city, and she was flabbergasted, letting loose a string of questions: Can God hear you if you pray in a whisper? Can you pray in bed? Can you pray on the bus? She told me of a new Christian she knew in Mongolia who once prayed, "Hello God. It's me, [name], oldest daughter of [name] and [name], my address is [address] . . ." After all, with so many people in the world praying, how could God possibly know who she was?

Not only do we have a God who knows us and hears our prayers, but we also pray to the Son of God, the great High Priest who intercedes for us! Jesus prays for us in accord with the Father's will, even when our own requests and desires are misguided. He speaks our hearts to the Father even when we don't have words and what comes out of our mouths is mere groaning. (At times my husband and I have literally groaned together in prayer, acknowledging with moans that our hurts and desires are deep and words have fallen short.) There is no international prayer exchange rate, no offering or gift to God that promises our requests will be granted. But we have more than a spiritual doctor who may or may not fix a problem for a price. We have a spiritual Father who has both all power and all grace and who, in infinite wisdom, will hear all prayers and answer as He knows is best.

ARTICLE 2:
WHY DID JESUS COME?

■ ■ ■

". . . And in Jesus Christ, His only Son, our Lord . . ."

▌▌ CATECHISM REFERENCE

And in Jesus Christ, His only Son, our Lord, who was conceived by the Holy Spirit, born of the Virgin Mary, suffered under Pontius Pilate, was crucified, died and was buried. He descended into hell. The third day He rose again from the dead. He ascended into heaven and sits at the right hand of God, the Father Almighty. From thence He will come to judge the living and the dead.

What does this mean? I believe that Jesus Christ, true God, begotten of the Father from eternity, and also true man, born of the Virgin Mary, is my Lord, who has redeemed me, a lost and condemned person, purchased and won me from all sins, from death, and from the power of the devil; not with gold or silver, but with His holy, precious blood and with His innocent suffering and death, that I may be His own and live under Him in His kingdom and serve Him in everlasting righteousness, innocence, and blessedness, just as He is risen from the dead, lives and reigns to all eternity. This is most certainly true.[9]

OPENING PRAYER

INTRODUCTION QUESTION

If you could eat dinner with any one person (past or present), who would you want to eat with? Why?

OPENING DISCUSSION

We might take the answers to the following questions for granted but much of the world doesn't. Consider carefully how you would respond and explain the answers to someone else.

- Can I know God? How?

....

....

....

- Does God want to know me? Why?

....

....

....

....

▪ REASON 1: JESUS CAME SO WE COULD KNOW GOD.

Read **John 1:14–18.**
How can we know God?

....

....

....

What do these verses show about God's desire to know us and be known by us?

....

....

....

APPLICATION

What does this mean about the value of people? this world? you?

....

....

....

Read **John 14:5–14.**
How does Jesus describe the relationship between Him and His Father?

....

....

....

....

According to these verses, why is faith in Jesus necessary?

....

....

....

....

....

....

DIGGING DEEPER

John 14:13–14 can be easily misunderstood to suggest "in Jesus' name, amen" is a magical formula for making sure our prayers are answered as we wish them to be. What does it really mean to pray "in Jesus' name?" (Consider: What would it mean to give a donation in someone else's name or sign a document in their name?)

....

....

....

....

What does Jesus say is the end goal of doing for us what we ask in His name?

....

....

....

....

....

....

▪▪ REASON 2: HE CAME TO SAVE US FROM SIN.

> **For there is no distinction: for all have sinned and fall short of the glory of God.** (ROMANS 3:22–23)

> **For the wages of sin is death.** (ROMANS 6:23)

> **For Christ also suffered once for sins, the righteous for the unrighteous, that He might bring us to God.**
>
> (1 PETER 3:18)

How does **1 Peter 3:18** describe the result of our salvation? In what way is this the same and different from saying, "You must believe in Jesus so you don't go to hell"?

....

....

....

....

Read **Romans 1:1–4**.
Why did Jesus need to be both man and God in order to die to save us?

....

....

....

....

What is the greatest proof of Jesus' divinity (**v. 4**)?

....

....

....

....

For God so loved the world, that He gave His only Son, that whoever believes in Him should not perish but have eternal life. (JOHN 3:16)

What was God's motive for saving us?

....

....

....

....

Who receives salvation and eternal life?[10]

....

....

....

....

....

DIGGING DEEPER

This is the most basic tenet of Christianity and one we know well, but how would you explain to someone what it means to *believe* in Jesus? What exactly do we have to believe about Him? How much does someone have to know to be saved? What other words could we use to explain *believe?*

....

....

....

....

....

....

APPLICATION

Speak the Gospel to the person next to you by reading this paraphrase of John 3:16 and putting his or her name in each blank. Rejoice in this wonderful truth!

For God so loved .... *that He gave His one and only Son, that if* .... *believes in Him,* .... *will not perish but* .... *will have eternal life.*

Look at the Second Article of the Creed, which summarizes who Jesus is (names and titles for Him, His divinity and humanity) and what He did to save us (His suffering, death, resurrection, and ascension).

And in Jesus Christ, His only Son, our Lord,

who was conceived by the Holy Spirit,

born of the Virgin Mary,

suffered under Pontius Pilate,

was crucified, died and was buried.

He descended into hell.

The third day He rose again from the dead.

He ascended into heaven

and sits at the right hand of God, the Father Almighty.

From thence He will come to judge the living and the dead.

Below are some common misunderstandings about Jesus.[11] Answer each misconception, using one or more Bible verses from this lesson or by referencing other Bible passages. Consider also

61

which phrase from the Creed you would use to answer these statements.

1. Jesus was only a good teacher. He wasn't God.

2. God could never understand our human life and experience.

3. God is too great and distant for humans to ever know conclusively who He is or what He is like.

4. There is no way God could ever accept me.

5. All faiths are the same. There are many ways to find God.

■■ PRAYER PROMPT

Pray in partners, using the words of Ephesians 3:16–19 and putting the other person's name in the blank.

I pray that out of God's great riches He may strengthen .... with power through His Spirit in ....'s inner being, so that Christ may dwell in ....'s heart through faith.

And I pray that .... would be rooted and built up in love.

I pray that .... may have power, together with all Christians, to know how wide and long and high and deep is the love of Christ.

And I pray that .... may know this love that is beyond knowing—so that .... may be filled with all the fullness of God.

▐▬ HYMN

God Loved the World So That He Gave

God loved the world so that He gave
His only Son the lost to save,
That all who would in Him believe
Should everlasting life receive.

Christ Jesus is the ground of faith,
Who was made flesh and suffered death;
All then who trust in Him alone
Are built on this chief cornerstone.

God would not have the sinner die;
His Son with saving grace is nigh;
His Spirit in the Word declares
That we in Christ are heaven's heirs.

Be of good cheer, for God's own Son
Forgives all sins which you have done;
And, justified by Jesus' blood,
Your Baptism grants the highest good.

If you are sick, if death is near,
This truth your troubled heart can cheer:
Christ Jesus saves your soul from death;
That is the firmest ground of faith.

Glory to God the Father, Son,
And Holy Spirit, Three in One!
To You, O blessèd Trinity,
Be praise now and eternally! (*LSB* 571)

To Know and Be Known

Long ago, at many times and in many ways, God spoke to our fathers by the prophets, but in these last days He has spoken to us by His Son. (HEBREWS 1:1–2)

When I was preparing to serve as an overseas missionary, one of my primary worries was not having the answers to people's questions. After all, my position was as a Bible teacher. Certainly I needed to know how to answer my students' questions so they could understand and know who God is! What would they think of my faith and witness if I didn't have answers for them? But perhaps the better question would have been to ask myself, What would they think of the Christian faith if I taught them that faith meant cerebral knowledge and perfect understanding and that it was my answers that could convey salvation?

God chose to accomplish the salvation of the world through the incarnation. He had already revealed Himself to His people through the Word and the prophets. They knew about Him. Yet the full revelation was given in the flesh, face-to-face. God's act of salvation was fleshy, earthy, relational. How could our witness be anything different?

How we share Jesus with other people says much about what we believe to be the nature of faith and the nature of God. If our Gospel proclamation is primarily about knowledge, then we are suggesting that faith is cerebral and God is most pleased by our theology. For those who love academic study and the pursuit of learning, this might be very comfortable. It puts faith into a neat package that we can wrap our minds around and present to others. For those who are less academically minded or who struggle deeply with questions and doubts about faith, this can feel like a heavy burden.

The night before my Taiwanese roommate was to be baptized, she came to talk to me because she was concerned that she still had questions about the Bible. She reasoned that she shouldn't be baptized if she didn't understand everything. In that moment, she didn't need me to answer all her questions; she needed me to assure her that I still have questions too, even after being a Christian my whole life. I reminded her that Baptism is not a graduation or an act of obedience that we perform for God. Baptism is God's gracious action to save us—not because we have earned it or grasped it but because Christ has done it for us. In Baptism, God "works forgiveness of sins, rescues from death and the devil, and gives eternal salvation to all who believe this"[12]—not to all who fully understand every aspect of theology. (Thank the Lord!)

It surprised me, when I served in Taiwan, to realize how disconcerting I found it to lose comfortable theological vocabulary. Whether I was talking about faith in simple English for second-language learners or in even simpler Chinese, I often had to forego the polysyllabic expressions that allowed me to believe I had a firm grasp on divine mysteries. I had to trust that the power of salvation came not from my eloquence or theological understanding but from the power of the cross. As Paul wrote to the Corinthian Church:

> I, when I came to you, brothers, did not come proclaiming to you the testimony of God with lofty speech or wisdom. For I decided to know nothing among you except Jesus Christ and Him crucified. And I was with you in weakness and in fear and much trembling, and my speech and my message were not in plausible words of wisdom, but in demonstration of

the Spirit and of power, so that your faith might not rest in the wisdom of men but in the power of God. (1 CORINTHIANS 2:1–5)

This reliance on God's power rather than our knowledge is deeply freeing. It allows all the saints to be part of God's mission to speak the Gospel to the world, rather than reserving this most important Christian work for only the scholars and seminary graduates. To be a missionary, both abroad and among people we see every day, is to know and love Jesus and to know and love people who don't yet know Jesus. This doesn't negate the importance of study or good theology. None of us wants to put up barriers to the Gospel by our own ignorance or misunderstanding! But this truth puts our trust where it belongs—in God Himself and in the power of the cross and the empty tomb. "'Knowledge' puffs up, but love builds up. If anyone imagines that he knows something, he does not yet know as he ought to know. But if anyone loves God, he is known by God" (1 Corinthians 8:1–3).

It is also critical that just as the Gospel message itself is relational, so our sharing of the Gospel must happen in relationship. God's plan for salvation was relational: Jesus took on flesh, lived among people, and called individuals to take the Gospel to the ends of the earth. And the message of salvific reconciliation that we share is inherently relational: Christ offers a way for mankind to be reunited with the Father. In light of this, how could our evangelism be anything but relational? People know when they are a project, when we are seeking only to accomplish a task of conversion rather than to care for a person. On the other hand, true love and care for unbelievers cannot help but motivate passionate witness!

One of the hardest conversations I had in Taiwan was with my Chinese tutor. She was a Buddhist woman who had heard the Gospel for decades but didn't yet believe, and we often had faith conversations during my lessons. However, she had recently had a Christian friend who, when my teacher told her she would probably never become a follower of Jesus, gave up on the relationship. My teacher asked me if I was going to stop caring about our relationship if she told me she would never be a Christian. In words that could have only come from the Spirit, I told her with tears in my eyes, "I will always care about you, no matter what you believe. But because I care about you, I will always keep telling you about Jesus because I believe knowing Him is the greatest thing you could ever have." When I reached out to her for permission to include this story in this study, she told me she thinks often about this conversation and that my reply is what has allowed her to keep being friends with Christians in the years that have followed. I continue to pray that one day she, too, will know Jesus as Lord.

ARTICLE 3:
I BELIEVE
IN THE HOLY SPIRIT

■ ■ ■

"I believe in the Holy Spirit, the holy Christian church, the communion of saints, the forgiveness of sins, the resurrection of the body, and the life everlasting. Amen."

■ CATECHISM REFERENCE

What does this mean? I believe that I cannot by my own reason or strength believe in Jesus Christ, my Lord, or come to Him; but the Holy Spirit has called me by the Gospel, enlightened me with His gifts, sanctified and kept me in the true faith. In the same way He calls, gathers, enlightens, and sanctifies the whole Christian church on earth, and keeps it with Jesus Christ in the one true faith.[13]

▪▪ OPENING PRAYER

▪▪ INTRODUCTION QUESTION

If you could choose one of these superpowers, which would you choose?

- Be able to speak any language
- Be able to travel instantly from one place to another
- Be able to know what other people are thinking

▪▪ KEY QUESTIONS

1. Why do we need the Holy Spirit?
2. How can I know if I have God's Spirit living in me?
3. How can I make someone else believe in Jesus?

▪▪ I. WHO IS THE HOLY SPIRIT?

A. The Holy Spirit is the Third Person of the Trinity: Father, Son and Holy Spirit.

B. The Bible describes specific roles the Holy Spirit has, but the triune God is always *united* in these works. The Nicene Creed reminds us that the Holy Spirit proceeds from (is sent by) the Father and the Son—the Trinity working in unity for our salvation.

1. The Holy Spirit's character is the same as God's character. Think of one example. God is ....

2. The Holy Spirit's will is the same as God's will. Think of one example. God's will is ....

3. The Holy Spirit's work is the same as God's work. Think of one example. God is working in the world to ....

▪▪ II. WHAT HAS THE HOLY SPIRIT DONE IN THE PAST?

A. Read **Genesis 1:1–3**. At the beginning, the Holy Spirit ....

B. Read **2 Peter 1:20–21**. Throughout the Bible, the Holy Spirit ....

C. Read **Luke 1:35**. Before Jesus' birth, the Holy Spirit ....

D. Read **Matthew 3:13–17**. At Jesus' Baptism, the Holy Spirit ....

E. Read **Luke 4:1, 14**. During Jesus' ministry, the Holy Spirit ....

F. Read **Acts 2:1–11**. After Jesus returned to heaven, the Holy Spirit ....

G. Read **Psalm 143:10; Psalm 51:10–11;** and **Psalm 139:7**. Was the Holy Spirit present in the world and in believers before Pentecost? ....

⠇⠇ III. WHAT DOES THE HOLY SPIRIT DO NOW?

Read **John 16:7–15**. What did Jesus tell His disciples about the sending of the Holy Spirit and the Spirit's work? Why is it to their (and our!) advantage that Jesus is no longer walking on this earth?

....

....

....

....

A. If you are a believer, some of the Spirit's work is *already done!* Only by the Holy Spirit's work through the Word and Sacraments can we say,...
(1 Corinthians 12:3).

B. If you are a believer, some of this work is *still being done.*

> **But the fruit of the Spirit is love, joy, peace, patience, kindness, goodness, faithfulness, gentleness, self-control; against such things there is no law. And those who belong to Christ Jesus have crucified the flesh with its passions and desires. If we live by the Spirit, let us also keep in step with the Spirit.**
>
> (GALATIANS 5:22–25)

Why do you think the Bible describes this as "fruit"?

....

....

....

....

....

IV. HOW DOES THE HOLY SPIRIT COME TO US?

Read **Acts 2:38** and **Luke 11:13**. What answers do these verses give to this question?

....

....

....

....

....

KEY POINTS TO REMEMBER

1. We *can't explain everything* about the Spirit or limit how and when He works. He is God. He is free to work how He wants to work (John 3:8).

2. The Holy Spirit is a *gift* from God. We can't tell Him what to do. We can't do anything to deserve Him or His work in us (Galatians 3:2–5, 14).

3. The Spirit always works *through the Word of God*. If you want more peace, joy, and confidence in God, read God's Word. If you want to understand more of God's Word, pray for the Spirit's help (John 6:63).

4. The Spirit is always united with the Father and Son. *God is ONE*. Don't try to separate the Trinity. The Spirit is always doing the Father's work and always pointing to Jesus (John 14:26).

APPLICATION

Now go back to the three key questions with which we opened the lesson. Answer these, using what we studied about the Holy Spirit.

1. Why do we need the Holy Spirit?

....

....

....

....

2. How can I know if I have God's Spirit living in me?

....

....

....

....

3. How can I make someone else believe in Jesus?

....

....

....

....

PRAYER PROMPTS

• *Praise God for the gifts of the Spirit in history and in your life.*
• *Pray for the fruit of the Spirit to overflow in your life and church.*
• *Pray for the Holy Spirit's work in the lives of people you know who don't yet know Jesus.*

HYMN

Come, Holy Ghost, God and Lord

Come, Holy Ghost, God and Lord,
With all Your graces now outpoured
On each believer's mind and heart;
Your fervent love to them impart.
Lord, by the brightness of Your light
In holy faith Your Church unite;
From ev'ry land and ev'ry tongue
This to Your praise, O Lord, our God, be sung:
Alleluia, alleluia!

Come, holy Light, guide divine,
Now cause the Word of life to shine.
Teach us to know our God aright
And call Him Father with delight.
From ev'ry error keep us free;
Let none but Christ our master be
That we in living faith abide,
In Him, our Lord, with all our might confide.
Alleluia, alleluia!

Come, holy Fire, comfort true,
Grant us the will Your work to do
And in Your service to abide;
Let trials turn us not aside.
Lord, by Your pow'r prepare each heart,
And to our weakness strength impart
That bravely here we may contend,
Through life and death to You, our Lord, ascend.
Alleluia, alleluia! (*LSB* 497)

How Can I Make Them Believe?

There was never a need for me or any of our pastors or church leaders to tell Asian Christians that they should share the Gospel with their friends, family, and co-workers. Their question was simply, How? As people who had personally known life without Jesus and experienced the transformative power of the Gospel, there was nothing they wanted more than for those they loved to experience the same transformation. The details were different for each person, of course—a seven-year-old boy praying each week in Sunday School for his father to come to faith; a young woman sharing the Gospel with a co-worker over lunch, even though it put them both at risk in their workplace; an older woman bringing the young man who sold fruit in her neighborhood to Bible study—but the ardent desire to see others come to faith was the same.

So when I posed the question to my Bible study class, "How can you make someone else believe in Jesus?" it caused quite a flurry of responses. People suggested many strategies for timing, tone, Scripture references, apologetics arguments, cultural connection points . . . until finally I had to cut off the discussion and simply say, "You can't." There was a stunned silence before we began to unpack this together, but as we discussed how only God has the power to give faith, the relief in the room was palpable. Certainly, this theological truth didn't take away all of their concerns and questions, but the burden was lifted. The responsibility of saving the world was back on God's shoulders.

The knowledge that only God can give saving faith doesn't take away the struggle and heartache that comes with deeply longing for someone else to come to faith. I have often prayed for people I love who don't trust in Jesus (including my dear Chinese teacher) and pleaded, "Lord, why won't You just give them faith? I know You can. I know You love them even more than I do and desire them to be saved, as You do all people. I know You can break down the barriers in their hearts and open them up to the Gospel. Just do it!" And there's no simple answer to these pleas and questions. Why does God do this work of faith quickly in some hearts while allowing others to wrestle with doubt and questions for decades before coming to faith? Why was I born into a Christian family in a country where Christianity is widespread and religious freedom is protected, and others I know were born into atheist families in countries with high levels of persecution? I don't know. But I do know that trusting that faith is God's to create and sustain is the only thing that makes mission possible.

When I traveled to churches while on summer furlough to present about mission work in Asia, people often treated me like either an odd anomaly or a super-Christian. I often heard people say things like "I could never do what you're doing." What I struggled to help people understand, though, is that serving as an overseas missionary had more to do with recognizing my weaknesses, my limits, and my dependency than it did with any power, confidence, or courage. Because the mission is God's, the power to accomplish this mission is His also!

> What then is Apollos? What is Paul? Servants through whom you believed, as the Lord assigned to each. I planted, Apollos watered, but God gave the growth. (1 Corinthians 3:5–6)

This missional power is not uniquely given to some subset of Christians who have particular piety or a particular calling. The same Spirit who hovered over the waters at creation, who caused the incarnation, and who moved among the early apostles lives in each one of us who confesses Jesus Christ as Lord. All who have been baptized and believe "receive the gift of the Holy Spirit. For the promise is for you and for your children and for all who are far off, everyone whom the Lord our God calls to Himself" (Acts 2:38–39).

An understanding of this gift of the Holy Spirit and His power and work is the greatest comfort we can give to believers seeking to engage in God's mission. First of all, mission-minded Christians have to be rooted in the knowledge that their own faith is a gift of God, "the founder and perfecter of our faith" (Hebrews 12:2). This is a comfort to rely on when we feel weak in faith, an assurance that our own belief is no accident of birth or culture, and a guard against pride in our own understanding or confidence. But it is also critical for all who would seek to share their faith with others to acknowledge that only God can give faith. This truth gives hope and perseverance to the believer witnessing to the person who seems least likely to ever believe, courage to the Christian who feels most unsure of her own witness, and peace to every Christian at the end of the day, trusting that this mission—along with every other part of life, material and spiritual—is in the loving, nail-scarred hands of our Savior.

ARTICLE 3:
I BELIEVE
IN THE CHURCH

■ ■ ■

"I believe in . . . the holy Christian church, the communion of saints . . ."

■ CATECHISM REFERENCE

202. What is the Church?

It is the body of Christ—that is, all people whom the Spirit, by the Means of Grace, has gathered to Christ in faith throughout the world. . . .

Note: The Creed in its original words speaks of the Church as "catholic" (universal)—that is, existing throughout all time and throughout the world, including people who confess and believe in Jesus Christ from every background ("people and nation,"

Revelation 5:9). Another way to say this is to speak of the "Christian Church."

While the word *Church,* properly speaking, refers to all those who believe in Christ, it is also used in other ways (such as a building, a congregation, a denomination). The word *church* is used for such things because confessing Christians are found within them.[14]

▪ OPENING PRAYER

▪ INTRODUCTION QUESTION

Talk briefly about a time you either felt strongly like you belonged or felt strongly like an outsider.

....

....

....

....

....

▪ OPENING DISCUSSION

What does *church* mean? What about *Church*? (See notes on the last page of this lesson, as well as the catechism reference above.)

....

....

....

....

....

▐▪ I. CHURCH = A BUILDING MADE OF PEOPLE

Key truth: God lives with and in His Church.
Read **Ephesians 2:11–22**.

A. **Verses 19–22** compare believers to what three things? What benefit comes from each?

Christians are...	What benefit(s) does this give us?

B. In **verses 20–22**, Paul describes a building. Draw this building on the next page. As you do, think about these questions: What kind of building is it? What's the foundation of the building? Who is included in the building? What's the most important part of the building? Who lives inside this building?

DIGGING DEEPER

In the Holy Christian Church, we are not divided into Jews and Gentiles. What divisions do we artificially make between our-selves within the body of believers?

....

....

....

....

....

∎ II. CHURCH = THE BODY OF CHRIST

Key truth: God has given each person gifts and united us with Christ as our head. God uses all of us working together with our varied gifts to accomplish His purposes.

Read **Romans 12:3–8**.

A. What does the image of a body add to our understanding of the Church?

....

....

....

....

....

B. How does this body have both unity and diversity?

....

....

....

....

....

APPLICATION

What gifts has God given you as part of the Body of Christ? It could be something in this list (Romans 12:6–8) or something else. Talk in a group of two or three people and help one another answer.

....

....

....

▐▪ III. CHURCH = THE BRIDE OF CHRIST

Key truth: God loves the Church deeply. Jesus makes the Church holy.

Read **Ephesians 5:25–33**.

A. How did Jesus make the Church holy?

....

....

....

....

B. What does God see when He looks at the Church? How is this like or unlike what you see when you look at the Church?

....

....

....

C. What does Jesus continue to do for the Church? (See **v. 29**.) What do you think that means?

....

....

....

....

The Church is not made of perfect people, but of people who admit their sin, depend on God's grace, and forgive one another.

- Hard news: This means people in the Church will fail us at times. You will be hurt by others, if you haven't already. The witness of the Church to the world is flawed and broken.

- Good news: This means that even though you are not perfect, you are welcome in God's Church! This also means the power and holiness of the Church is from God—not us. Jesus died to make the Church holy, and His Spirit is working to make her more and more godly!

DIGGING DEEPER

Why do you think we say in the Creed that we *believe* in "the holy Christian church"? We can see our churches. We can see the worshipers beside us in the pews. Why do we need faith?

....
....
....
....
....
....

IV. BEING THE CHURCH

Consider: How would you explain what it looks like to be the Church? When do we come together? What do we do when we come together? (Imagine someone asked you not "What do you do at church?" but "What does the Church do?")

....
....
....
....
....
....

Therefore, brothers, since we have confidence to enter the holy places by the blood of Jesus, by the new and living way that He opened for us through the curtain, that is, through His flesh, and since we have a great priest over the house of God, let us draw near with a true heart in full assurance of faith, with our hearts sprinkled clean from an evil conscience and our bodies washed with pure water. Let us hold fast the confession of our hope without wavering, for He who promised is faithful. And let us consider how to stir up one another to love and good works, not neglecting to meet together, as is the habit of some, but encouraging one another, and all the more as you see the Day drawing near. (HEBREWS 10:19–25)

A. What things do these verses say the Church does together?

....

....

....

....

B. What does it look like to stir up other believers to love and good works?

....

....

....

....

....

C. Why do you think the writer says we must not give up meeting together?

....

....

....

....

....

> **Let the word of Christ dwell in you richly, teaching and admonishing one another in all wisdom, singing psalms and hymns and spiritual songs, with thankfulness in your hearts to God.** (COLOSSIANS 3:16)

D. What things do these verses say the Church does together?

....

....

....

....

....

> **And they devoted themselves to the apostles' teaching and the fellowship, to the breaking of bread and the prayers.** (ACTS 2:42)

E. What things do these verses say the Church does together?

....

....

....

....

....

DIGGING DEEPER

Of all the activities you listed from these three passages, which ones are done in worship on Sunday? Which might be better done in small groups or one-on-one? (Some might go in more than one place.)

LARGE GROUP	SMALL GROUP	ONE-ON-ONE

Church is not a weekly one-hour activity—it is people who are following Jesus together and living every day for His kingdom and His mission.

APPLICATION

What can we do to *be* the Church at times other than Sunday?

▓ PRAYER PROMPTS

• *Pray for God's Church to grow here and around the world.*
• *Pray for God to make the Church more united.*
• *Pray for God to help us love the Church and to grant us grace to forgive and heal from hurts that have happened in our churches. Pray also for God to call those who have hurt us to confession and absolution.*
• *Pray for God to show you your gifts and help you use them in the Church.*

▓ NOTES ON CHURCH

1. The word *church* sometimes refers to a building.

2. The word *church* sometimes refers to a group of people who meet regularly in one place to share God's Word and Sacraments and worship Him.

3. The word *Church* (or *the Church*) means "all believers in Jesus in every time and place."

    a. This Church is *invisible*. We don't know who has faith; only God can judge.

    b. This Church is *infallible*. Individual churches and denominations may come and go. God's Church will last forever (Matthew 16:16–18).

▓ HYMN

Church of God, Elect and Glorious

> Church of God, elect and glorious,
> Holy nation, chosen race;

91

Called as God's own special people,
Royal priests and heirs of grace:
Know the purpose of your calling,
Show to all His mighty deeds;
Tell of love that knows no limits,
Grace that meets all human needs.

God has called you out of darkness
Into His most marv'lous light;
Brought His truth to life within you,
Turned your blindness into sight.
Let your light so shine around you
That God's name is glorified
And all find fresh hope and purpose
In Christ Jesus crucified.

Once you were an alien people,
Strangers to God's heart of love;
But He brought you home in mercy,
Citizens of heav'n above.
Let His love flow out to others,
Let them feel a Father's care;
That they too may know His welcome
And His countless blessings share.

Church of God, elect and holy,
Be the people He intends;
Strong in faith and swift to answer
Each command your Master sends:
Royal priests, fulfill your calling
Through your sacrifice and prayer;
Give your lives in joyful service—
Sing His praise, His love declare. (*LSB* 646)

Being the Church

One of the most powerful things I learned from Asian Christians was to see in new ways what it looks like to be the Church. One of the places I lived was a large urban center where the average age of the population was under thirty and someone who had lived there a year or two was considered a local. It was a transient population of young people looking to make it in business, technology, or trade—people from all over the country who had left their families and hometowns to seek dreams of wealth and success, fighting for these dreams amid fierce competition and a high-stress work culture. As you might imagine, this resulted in a city of both hopeful energy and deep brokenness. There was a pervading sense of lostness and isolation among so many people that I met, people searching for community and stability in a city where everyone was a local and so no one was.

When you add to the unique nature of this city a long-standing cultural emphasis on community, collective identity, and interdependence, you have an environment ripe for strong church community. Many new believers—or not-yet believers—came to the church looking for a place to belong and a sense of identity. And when a person became a believer, transferring his or her loyalty and identity to Christ and His household, the new believer often displayed a beautifully wholehearted devotion. I think of my Friday Bible study group that gathered week after week, arriving at church at 7 p.m. straight from work and facing an hour-long metro commute home at the end of the night. They were so eager to learn and grow in faith despite their weekend weariness. I think of a woman who came to me one Sunday morning asking how to make a special offering, overjoyed that she had been given a bonus at work and so had more money to offer back to God. I think of believers who risked everything economically for the sake of the Gospel—losing jobs for refusing to dishonestly report company profits, threatened with the loss of a pension for publicly confessing Christ. I think of parents who risked their kids' futures in a highly competitive society by homeschooling or enrolling in unofficial Christian schools rather than putting their children into public school classrooms where they would be indoctrinated in atheism—and conversely I think of parents who intentionally placed their children into these public schools, knowing how challenging this environment would be for them, yet believing it was essential for these classrooms to have Christian children in them who would witness to their classmates.

Most of all, I think of the ways believers took care of one another, truly acting as if the people next to them in the pews were blood brothers and sisters. We commonly addressed one another as "Sister Emily" or "Brother Jacob." I frequently arrived an hour before the worship service began to find pairs of people sharing with each other and praying together in the sanctuary. When a Christian was struggling with pressure from unbelieving parents who wanted him or her to marry an unbeliever or a non-Christian spouse who didn't want his or her child brought to church, other believers would often go with that person to meet with these family members and speak on behalf of their fellow Christian.

One very practical example of this Christian brotherhood was care for the hospitalized. While local medical care was of similar quality to that in the United States, hospitals provided for only medical needs, not any of the other daily needs of their patients. When someone was hospitalized, a cot would be put up at the foot of his or her bed for a family member to stay. This family member was responsible for providing the patient with meals, bringing toiletries, and even helping administer medication. My husband and I learned this when an elderly American pastor who had come to serve with us was hospitalized, and the nurses asked—much to our surprise—which of us was going to spend the night by his bedside. While neither of us ended up sleeping on a hospital cot, we did retrieve comfortable clothes for him from his apartment, bring him a supply of bottled water, and help with buying meals and hygiene items from convenience stores in the hospital. In a humorous turn of events, when two of his children came the next day, they were shooed out after the visiting hour ended, at which point the nurses asked where I was so I could keep caring for him!

In our city, however, where many people were far away from family, church brothers and sisters took on these roles. When one Asian sister was hospitalized, other young people in the congregation took turns being with her night and day, buying and cooking food for her, and making sure she was never alone. I went to visit and was surprised to find four or five other church members in the room, not just there to bring flowers and a greeting but there to minister with their presence. When a fellow American needed hospital care, not only did church members take turns staying with her, but one Christian brother also accompanied her throughout the whole hospital stay to act as a translator and make sure she understood everything that was going on. After all, this is exactly what one would do if a biological brother or sister were in need!

My Buddhist Chinese tutor in Taiwan once commented on photographs she had seen of me and other American teachers at our school, remarking that we seemed to have particularly close relationships. She asked if this closeness stemmed from being fellow Americans or from being Christian. I told her quite honestly that I frequently saw other Westerners in Taiwan and felt no sense of connection to them. (In fact, many who have lived as expatriates in another country will probably tell you there is an odd habit that expats have of trying to avoid one another in public as they each seek to blend in with the local culture.) But the connection between fellow Christians—whether from the same culture or not—is a powerful bond indeed. After I confirmed what she already suspected, my teacher commented thoughtfully, "I have been a Buddhist my entire life, and I have never felt such a connection to other Buddhists."

The Holy Christian Church is essential to what it means to be believers. It is not an added perk for those of us who have a relationship with Jesus, as if faith were about me and Jesus and getting into heaven, and Christian community was a nice add-on. The Church is an essential and inevitable part of being added to the family of God by faith. If we believe in the Father, we have new brothers and sisters. If we are baptized into Christ, we are baptized into His Body. If we identify as Christian, we are permanently bonded to all others who share this name and identity.

ARTICLE 3: FOREVER WITH GOD

■ ■ ■

"I believe . . . in the forgiveness of sins, the resurrection of the body, and the life everlasting. Amen."

■ CATECHISM REFERENCE

204. What is the forgiveness of sins?

God promises that, for Christ's sake, He will not hold our many sins against us.

205. Why does God forgive our sins?

God forgives our sins because He is merciful and because of Christ's atoning sacrifice for all sinners.

223. *What happens to me as a Christian when I die?*

When I die, the God-given unity of my body and spirit will be broken. I will immediately be in the presence of Christ, in heaven, but my body will remain in the grave until the resurrection.

224. *What will happen to me when I am raised from the dead on the Last Day?*

I will enjoy being with Christ in His new creation, in body and soul, forever.

225. *What will happen to this world after we Christians are raised from the dead?*

The present creation, like our own bodies, will be set free from its bondage to corruption, and God will create a new heaven and a new earth.[15]

▋▪ OPENING PRAYER

▋▪ INTRODUCTION QUESTION

Share a Bible verse you want read at your deathbed or funeral. Why did you pick this verse?

....

....

....

....

....

....

▪ OPENING DISCUSSION

Why is it important that this phrase in the Creed includes both "the resurrection of the body" *and* "the life everlasting"? What is missing if we talk only about eternal life in heaven and not bodily resurrection?

....

....

....

....

....

▪ I. THE FORGIVENESS OF SINS

Although "forgiveness of sins" is placed in the Third Article of the Creed, it's closely tied to each of the articles and to the work of each person of the Trinity. It is forgiveness—the removal of our sins, which lead to death—that makes possible everlasting life with God. (See Romans 6:23.)

A. *The Father*

God's nature as Father and Creator makes forgiveness both necessary and possible.

1. Regarding our need for forgiveness, read **Malachi 1:6; Hosea 11:1–7**; and **Romans 1:18–23**. What do we owe to God as our Father and Creator? Could you ever fully live this out?

....

....

....

....

2. Regarding God's mercy to forgive, read **Isaiah 49:15–16; Isaiah 46:3–4**; and **Psalm 145:8–10**. Why can we trust that we have forgiveness from the Father?

....

....

....

....

....

B. The Son

God's mercy is given to us through the life, death, and resurrection of the Son.

Read **Philippians 2:8; Matthew 3:16–17**; and **Romans 8:1–4, 14–17**. How did Jesus fulfill the debt we owe to God, our Father and Creator? What does Romans 8 say about how Christ has taken away our sin and what this means for our relationship with God?

....

....

....

....

....

C. The Spirit

As the Small Catechism explains, we "receive this forgiveness through faith, that is, by believing the promise of the Gospel."[16] It is the work of the Spirit to give us such faith.

1. How do **Romans 8:14–17** and **Galatians 4:4–7** talk about the work of the Spirit?

....

....

....

....

....

2. How and when do we receive this forgiveness of sins? Read **Acts 2:38; Matthew 26:28;** and **John 20:22–23.**

....

....

....

....

3. In what ways is it comforting to repeatedly see, taste, and hear our forgiveness in Word and Sacrament?

....

....

....

....

The forgiveness of sins powerfully impacts our lives here and now, as well as for eternity. How does this forgiveness affect the following:

1. Our relationship with God. Read **Hebrews 10:17–22.**

....

....

....

....

2. Our relationship with others. Read **Ephesians 4:31–32.**

....

....

3. Our sanctified life (the Spirit's work to make us more like Christ). Read **Hebrews 10:14.**

....

....

II: WHY DOES THE RESURRECTION MATTER?

But if there is no resurrection of the dead, then not even Christ has been raised. And if Christ has not been raised, then our preaching is in vain and your faith is in vain. (1 CORINTHIANS 15:13–14)

This is what the whole Apostles' Creed has been building to.

A. The First Article—God is our Father and Creator.

We were created to live forever in relationship with God. Read **Genesis 2:16–17** and **Romans 6:23.** Why did death enter the world?
Death came because of ....

B. The Second Article—Jesus lived, died, and rose for us.

Read **John 10:10.** Why did Jesus come?
He came to bring ....

C. The Third Article—the Holy Spirit works faith in Christ, which grants forgiveness.

Read **Ephesians 1:13–14.** What is the relationship between the Spirit and eternal life?

....

....

....

....

....

THE STORY OF THE BIBLE

We were created for life with God. Sin separated us from God and brought suffering and death. Jesus came to reconcile the world to God and give eternal, resurrected life.

DIGGING DEEPER

Why is it that most people fight against death or fear it? When someone we love dies, why do we feel pain and sadness, anger and denial? Why do most cultures believe in some kind of life after death?

III. THE RESURRECTION OF THE DEAD

A. Read **John 5:28–29.** Who will rise again?

....

....

....

....

B. Keep looking at **John 5:28–29,** and read **Hebrews 9:27–28**. What will be different for believers and unbelievers at the resurrection?

....

....

....

....

C. Read **Job 19:25–27.** Some people argue that resurrection is only spiritual. Other people believe in reincarnation. How does what Job says contradict both these ideas?

....

....

....

....

IV. THE LIFE EVERLASTING

A. Read **John 17:3** and **John 3:36.** How do believers have everlasting life right now?

....

....

....

....

B. Read **Ecclesiastes 12:7** and **Luke 23:39–43.** What happens as soon as a believer dies?

....

....

....

....

C. Read **1 Corinthians 15:21–23, 42–44,** and **51–53.** What will happen when Jesus comes back at the end of the world?

....

....

....

....

DIGGING DEEPER

Resurrection is almost too incredible to believe. Everything we see on earth ends in death. What proof do we have that there is life after death?

....

....

....

D. What will this eternal life be like?

> **And I heard a loud voice from the throne saying, "Behold, the dwelling place of God is with man. He will dwell with them, and they will be His people, and God Himself will be with them as their God. He will wipe away every tear from their eyes, and death shall be no more, neither shall there be mourning, nor crying, nor pain anymore, for the former things have passed away."** (REVELATION 21:3–4)

....

....

....

....

E. What will be the best part of eternal life?

....

....

....

....

....

:: PRAYER PROMPTS

- *Praise God for the gift of eternal life, now and in heaven.*
- *Pray for those who are sick and dying and those who love and care for them. Pray for the echo of Jesus' empty tomb to ring out loudly in their hearts.*
- *Pray for grace to live each day in light of eternity.*

:: HYMN

Jesus Lives! The Victory's Won

> Jesus lives! The vict'ry's won!
> Death no longer can appall me;
> Jesus lives! Death's reign is done!
> From the grave will Christ recall me.
> Brighter scenes will then commence;
> This shall be my confidence.
>
> Jesus lives! To Him the throne
> High above all things is given.
> I shall go where He is gone,
> Live and reign with Him in heaven.
> God is faithful; doubtings, hence!
> This shall be my confidence.

Jesus lives! For me He died,
Hence will I, to Jesus living,
Pure in heart and act abide,
Praise to Him and glory giving.
All I need God will dispense;
This shall be my confidence.

Jesus lives! I know full well
Nothing me from Him shall sever.
Neither death nor pow'rs of hell
Part me now from Christ forever.
God will be my sure defense;
This shall be my confidence.

Jesus lives! And now is death
But the gate of life immortal;
This shall calm my trembling breath
When I pass its gloomy portal.
Faith shall cry, as fails each sense:
Jesus is my confidence!   (*LSB* 490)

But We'll See Jesus

Both of my grandmothers were storytellers, and both loved to repeat a collection of favorites. While I spent childhood chuckling about this, catching my brother or sister's eye across the dinner table as we both correctly guessed which story was about to come, I often found myself repeating these women's wisdom to my Bible study students in Asia. More than one class heard my Grandma Barz's adage "Now we're rich; maybe someday we'll have money," and more than one student (particularly those who were mothers or pastor's wives) asked to borrow a copy of her memoir, *Six and a Bonus.* But the story that came off my lips, that brought tears to my eyes as I struggled to comfort the students in front of me, was from my Grandma Stampfli.

Orgene Stampfli was a Lutheran teacher and loved to tell stories about her classes, especially stories about teaching the faith and relying on God's wisdom to know how to answer inquisitive young minds. Once, she told us, she had been talking with her students about heaven, and a little girl raised her hand and asked, "But what if someone got to heaven and found out her mother wasn't there?" Grandma said that at that moment, without missing a beat, a boy in the front row looked up at her and said, "But we'll see Jesus." And, she would say, in that one sentence was a sermon of wisdom.

I remember hearing (and rehearing) this story as I was growing up and smiling at the sweetness of the comment, but noticing that it always made my grandmother tear up. And then I stood in front of a class of first-generation Christians—young believers who had asked me to pray for ailing grandparents who refused to listen to the Gospel, older believers who knew their parents and grandparents before them had never known Jesus, women who had recently come to faith but had husbands and children who didn't yet believe. I stood in front of this group, talking about the beautiful hope of eternal life that is ours in Christ. I longed to give some comfort to those who had lost loved ones, and yet I knew I couldn't speak of salvation apart from faith in Christ. And so instead, I told my grandmother's story, tearing up myself now at the heartrending knowledge that there are people we know and love who will not be saved—and yet there will be no sadness or mourning in heaven because "we will see Jesus."

Too often, I'm afraid, when we talk about the promise of eternal life, we miss the whole point. Whether we're speculating about what it will feel like to be outside the bounds of time or wondering if our pets will be there or whether we're focusing on the scriptural promises of an end to crying, hunger, and pain, too often our descriptions leave the promise of dwelling in the presence of God to be an afterthought. But this is what salvation is all about.

I remember being taken aback when a class of ninth graders in Taiwan told me they weren't interested in eternal life. As one female student put it, "Life is beautiful because it's short. It's precious because we only have so much time to make the most of." I wasn't sure how to respond. How could I convince them of the importance of faith in Jesus and salvation from sin if they not only didn't believe in an afterlife but didn't want one? Perhaps in part this student's comment was motivated by the naivete of youth. No teenager feels close to death, and it's easy to say you are content with a finite existence when you are just on the cusp of a lifetime of experiences. And yet, I had to realize that I wasn't here to sell students on their need for eternity. The promise of the Gospel is more than life after death. It's relationship. It's wholeness in the presence of God, knowing and being fully known, now and for eternity.

In the words of Revelation, the promise of the new heaven and new earth is this: "The dwelling place of God is *with* man. He will dwell *with* them, and they will be His people, and God Himself will be *with* them as their God" (21:3, emphasis mine). After all, the name of the Savior is Immanuel, "God with us." Christ died, "the righteous for the unrighteous, that He might bring us to God" (1 Peter 3:18). Christ's death and resurrection was not just to bring believers to a perfect wonderland in the sky; it was to bring us to God.

This is the climax of the Creed. This is the climax of the Gospel. This is the climax of our lives.

We will see Jesus.

Leader Guide

OVERVIEW
FOR LEADERS
■ ■ ■

Bible Study Aims

This study is designed to lead both new Christians and lifelong believers in an in-depth and practical study of the Apostles' Creed. While the words of this Creed are deeply familiar to most believers, the meaning and implications of this ancient statement of faith may not be something many Christians consider often or may be something they haven't studied since confirmation. Lessons lead participants through relevant Bible passages to draw out the meaning of the article being considered and include related material from Luther's Small and Large Catechisms. The application questions and discussion topics in each session are meant to help participants make connections between faith and daily life and to give them tools to share their faith when they encounter the questions of others. The prayers and hymns are included to focus participants' attention on the work of the Holy Spirit in our hearts and minds and to ask God's blessing on our time together. You may use the prayers provided, adapt them to your group's format, or use other prayers that suit your group's needs. Hymns can be sung or listened to from recorded versions, according to your group's structure and time frame.

Bible Study Format

This study is not lecture heavy. Certainly it is important for you to have a clear grasp of the material and an ability to guide people in understanding Scripture, but the bulk of the learning will come from participants reading and responding to the biblical texts directly and from group discussion. To aid in this learning format, it is recommended to divide participants into small groups, with table leaders who keep the conversation on track and take responsibility for directing uncertainties back to the instructor or to the pastor. Table leaders may be the same person throughout the length of the study or may be a different person for each session, according to the group's preference and design.

Before each session, you as the instructor should familiarize yourself with the lesson by doing the following:

- Ask God to guide your teaching that it may deepen the participants' understanding of the Creed and draw them and you closer to Himself.

- Read in advance the leader and participant materials.

- Review the section in the Small Catechism that relates to the article addressed in this lesson. If possible, review also the related section in the Large Catechism.

- Read all Bible verses referenced in the lesson, keeping the context of the verses in mind. Read also any notes and commentary about the verses in your study Bible.

While admittedly group discussion is less time efficient than teacher-delivered content, this interaction and personal application is what will make learning lasting and transformative. Even the most insightful preacher or teacher will never be able to specifically apply truths to each participant's life in the same way individuals make life connections from their own experiences. For believers to learn how to "read, mark, learn, and inwardly digest"[17] the words of Scripture, they must be given the time and guidance of small-group Bible study as a model for their own personal Bible reading.

When class time is limited, don't worry about finishing a full lesson each session. Simply study as much as you have time for and continue where you left off in the next class. It is much more important to allow time for the content to get to the hearts and minds of students than for the class to rush to get through all the material.

This study is arranged in two sections, divided between the participant and the leader. When used in small group Bible study, the leader is as much a participant as others at the table, so while you as the leader will be prepared to guide the group through discussion questions and will be equipped with suggested answers, you will also answer the questions, engage in discussion, and complete the workbook pages.

The participant section begins on page 25. These workbook-like pages provide space for writing directly in this book. Invite participants to take notes on their own answers as well as the comments of others, and encourage them to highlight and otherwise mark up this book to make it a unique and personal discovery of the Creed.

It will be important for participants to bring a study Bible and something to write with each time the group meets. Encourage them to write in their Bible, highlight, and underline passages and annotations that inform their study. God, in His Word, speaks to each of us personally and intends for us to take it to heart. Looking back later on highlighted passages and notes from previous Bible study can serve as a beautiful record of God's ongoing work to guide us into deeper knowledge of Him.

Lesson Format

This leader's guide follows a traditional leader-learner format and is presented in outline form. Leaders will facilitate by keeping discussion on track and, as much as possible, within the time frame of the session. Participants will engage in lessons via group discussion and by using the workbook section. All group members are encouraged to read the topical essays after each session to further their understanding and application of the information.

As the leader, open the study in prayer, asking God to guide your study and discussion, leading you all into deeper understanding of Him and His Word. Short scriptural prayers are provided to open the lesson, but you may add to this as desired.

This leader's guide includes the following:

1. **Objectives** are given for each lesson to keep you focused on key truths participants should take away from the study. You are encouraged to share these objectives with students so that they will be aware of where the class is going.

2. **Introduction questions** can be used to help students get to know one another and build a foundation of comfortable conversation before they dive into deeper questions of faith and personal life.

3. **Opening discussion** questions will help students begin to think about the key themes of the lesson and their meaning for our lives. These questions shouldn't be addressed in depth or brought to conclusive answers. They simply serve to hook students' attention and get them thinking about the theme of the lesson. By the end of the lesson, answers to these questions should be apparent to students.

4. **Bible readings** are paired with general **questions** about the text, **digging deeper** questions to challenge and stimulate thinking among more mature Christians, and **application questions** to connect the text to everyday thoughts and actions.

5. Every lesson concludes with ideas for closing **prayer time**. While it may sometimes be appropriate to do this prayer time as a whole class, allowing small groups to pray together often creates better student involvement, relationship building, and personal sharing. It also encourages believers to see prayer as not just a pastor- or teacher-led activity but something that every Christian is invited to do.

6. Each lesson has a supplemental **hymn** and **catechism references**. You may use these in class as you deem appropriate and helpful, or direct students to these texts for perusal at home. Hymns can be read or prayed aloud, listened to, or sung together as the setting allows.

7. The participant pages include an **introduction** to the Creed from Luther's Small Catechism, and **topical essays** drawing on the author's mission experiences follow each lesson. The catechetical material is to remind participants of the doctrinal and practical application of the Creed. The essays can be used as prereading or taken home as devotional follow-up. It is important for you, the leader, to read the introduction as part of your preparation before leading the first session of this study and to encourage participants to read this material as well. You may even want to hold an introductory session before beginning the study sessions. And you will benefit from reading the topical essays before each session so you may encourage students to read them as well.

Discussion may go beyond the scope of this book, and participants may have questions you are not comfortable answering. As much as possible, point participants to what we know of the triune God from the Bible, referencing study Bible notes as well as the Small and Large Catechisms. And always offer to speak to a pastor, then come back to the next session with additional information. While it may feel uncomfortable as a leader to not always have answers, these moments of not knowing provide opportunities to model how Christians respond when we don't understand elements of our faith—with prayer, use of Bible study resources, and learning from pastors and teachers. Hard questions also remind us that our salvation is not found in our own theological answers but in the gracious work of Christ on our behalf. We can celebrate and rest in the reality of who God is—infinitely great and beyond our understanding, and yet beautifully and sufficiently revealed to us in His Word.

Leader Guide

ARTICLE 1:
WHAT IS GOD LIKE?

■ ■ ■

*"I believe in God, the Father Almighty,
Maker of heaven and earth."*

▪▪ CATECHISM REFERENCE

What does this mean? I believe that God has made me and all creatures; that He has given me my body and soul, eyes, ears, and all my members, my reason and all my senses, and still takes care of them. He also gives me clothing and shoes, food and drink, house and home, wife and children, land, animals, and all I have. He richly and daily provides me with all that I need to support this body and life. He defends me against all danger and guards and protects me from all evil. All this He does only out of fatherly, divine goodness and mercy, without any merit or worthiness in me. For all this it is my duty to thank and praise, serve and obey Him.

This is most certainly true.[18]

▐ LESSON OBJECTIVES

By God's grace, we will

- consider the implications of God's identity as Creator for our own lives and for our interactions with others and the world;

- meditate on the great love and sacrificial forgiveness of God the Father; and

- examine our attitudes and actions toward others in light of their identity as brothers and sisters, either heirs of God's kingdom and His beloved children by Baptism in Christ Jesus, or lost siblings being sought after by our Father.

▐ OPENING PRAYER

Almighty God, Maker of the world and everything in it, Lord of heaven and earth, You are worthy of all praise! Thank You that, in Your mercy, You have created us as Your offspring and drawn near to us in Christ. Open our hearts and minds to hear from Your Word today that we might more deeply know You as Father and Creator and live as Your beloved children. Amen.

▐ REVIEW THE CATECHISM REFERENCE WITH THE CLASS.

▐ INTRODUCTION QUESTION

Choose one of the following questions to answer:

1. What does your name mean?

2. How did your parents pick your name?

3. What other names or nicknames do people call you?

▪ OPENING DISCUSSION

God is almighty (has all power) and He loves you as a father.

What would it mean for us if God were only powerful but not loving?

Such a god (much like gods of other religions) would be terrifying. If God were just powerful, He would be awe inspiring and deserving of worship, but there would be no opportunity or desire for relationship. Worship of such a god could only be out of fear of what he could and would do to us.

The Daoist temples that dot Taiwanese street corners are filled with images of such fear-inspiring gods. In Chiayi, where I lived, there is a Seven Levels of Hell Temple where people worship gods of hell, hoping to avoid ending up there. Such fear of evil powers invokes worship and devotion but no love or relationship.

What would it mean for us if God were only loving but not powerful?

Perhaps we in the West are more tempted to view God this way (only as baby Jesus, meek and mild), but such a god is of no help to us either. While sharing a message of only love sounds tolerant and comfortable, without power such love does us no good. Yes, such a god might want what is good for us, but he would have no power to accomplish it. In contrast, as Luther's explanation tells us, our God has power to provide all we need as well as to defend us from all evil and danger.

▪ I. GOD IS THE MAKER OF HEAVEN AND EARTH.

Read Acts 17:24–29.

A. Where did everything in the world come from?

Everything material and spiritual, everything ever created—even our daily lives and breath—is from God. We see immediately in Genesis 1 God's immense power to create everything from nothing by His Word.

B. In what ways is God still working in creation and our lives? On a scale from 1 to 10, how involved is He in the events of daily life?

God didn't create the world and then let it spin, as Deists would say. Paul says God is very involved in every part of daily life (Acts 17:26, 28). He is our source of life and being. He directs the times and places of our existence and the course of human history—even the lives of unbelievers are under His authority (see Ezra 1:1–2; John 19:10–11). As Luther tells us in his explanation, each bit of simple daily provision is God's work in our lives, as are His protection and defense moment by moment.

Challenge students with this second question. Often, we are tempted to see only minor involvement (the occasional answered prayer or rumored miracle), but Paul says God is fully and completely involved in every aspect of our lives. For one example of this deep knowledge of and involvement in our lives, see Psalm 139:1–16. All of our movements, thoughts, and words are known by God before we even live them out. God created our inmost being and wrote each of our days.

C. What is God's purpose for creating us and working in our lives?

His purpose is that people would seek Him and find Him (Acts 17:27). Eternal relationship with Himself is God's goal for us. The purpose of Christ's coming and saving work on the cross was to make this possible—to seek and save the lost and raise up to eternal life all who trust in Him (see John 6:39–40; Luke 19:10).

DIGGING DEEPER

Reread Acts 17:25.

1. Does God need you to do things for Him? What, then, does it mean to serve Him?

No, of course God doesn't need anything—although we often live our lives with a franticness that suggests God is depending upon us. Idols are dependent upon human beings, but the almighty God is not. When we talk about serving God, we mean keeping His Commandments and serving our neighbors.

2. Who does need your help? Why do we help others?

Our neighbors, who are also made and loved by God, do need our help. We love and serve others in response to the love God has shown us.

APPLICATION

God made everything. If you believe this fact, it changes how you view all of life! Below are six situations you might encounter in conversations with others.[19] How would you answer in each situation based on what we've read in Acts 17 or by referencing other Bible passages about God as our Creator?

Additional texts and explanation are provided below for leader reference. Encourage students to begin by applying what they have learned from Acts 17 and by teasing out the implications of God being our Creator and the Creator of all people and of this world. Then use the verses and notes provided in the answers to add depth to the conversation.

1. IF SOMEONE SAYS, "I DO NOT HAVE MUCH VALUE"?

You are precious! The God who made the whole world also made you (His offspring—His child). He knows you and is directing your life because He wants a relationship with you. Think about how much a work of art or a dish of food is worth if it is created by someone famous. Now consider what it means that you are the handiwork of the king of Creation (Psalm 139:13–16), created in the image and likeness of the triune God (Genesis 1:27; James 3:9)!

2. IF SOMEONE SAYS, "MY LIFE HAS NO MEANING"?

Nothing in your life is an accident. God created you and gave you life and being, directing your times and places with the purpose of bringing you into relationship with Him. God is intimately involved in your life, and His purpose for you is to know Him and become more like Him, to be conformed to the image of Jesus (Romans 8:29). As a follower of Jesus, every work and relationship you engage in has eternal significance as you walk in the good works God has prepared for you (Ephesians 2:10).

Certainly, our lives are marred by sin, and there are no easy responses to the things we each suffer as a result of our own sin and this sinful world. And yet God promises to work all things together for good (Romans 8:28). We can see as just one example from Scripture how God used years of suffering in Joseph's life to bring about the saving of his family and all Egypt from famine.

3. IF SOMEONE IS CONSIDERING ABORTING AN UNBORN CHILD?

Every child (and his or her mother!) is a creation of God, given life and breath by God's will, and created for relationship with Him (Psalm 139:13–16). God is the one who creates and directs life, not us. He gives life and breath to each of His offspring (Acts 17:25) and holds our times in His hands (Psalm 31:15). And while God does not need our service, our neighbor does. There are many good resources (for example, from Lutherans for Life) that explain the value of life and the responsibility of Christians to protect unborn lives. In this conversation, however, if talking to a desperate woman considering abortion, what may be most important is not what we say but what we do. If we are pro-life, how do we support the lives of mother, father, and child to make abortion not an attractive or necessary option? How do we comfort and assure a woman that she is not alone as she faces the challenges of pregnancy, childbirth, and parenthood?

> 4. IF SOMEONE DOESN'T CARE WHAT EFFECT HIS OR HER ACTIONS HAVE ON THE ENVIRONMENT?

The world is God's creation, and He is Lord of both heaven and earth. How can we disrespect and abuse this very good gift from our Creator, the earth over which we have been given dominion (Genesis 1:28)? We who believe in the resurrection of the dead and the new heaven and new earth should know the value the physical world has to God (Colossians 1:15–20).

> 5. IF SOMEONE SAYS, "I CAN DO ANYTHING I WANT TO. NOBODY HAS THE RIGHT TO TELL ME WHAT IS RIGHT OR WRONG"?

God is our Maker and our source of life and breath. He has authority over every part of creation. We don't belong to ourselves. God as both Father and Ruler has commanded repentance because the day is coming on which He will judge the world (Acts 17:30–31). Not only does God have all authority over our lives, but He has also put others in authority over us, including parents and rulers, as laid out in the Fourth Commandment. The power of these authorities comes from God, who has all power and authority over us as our Creator (Romans 13:1).

> 6. IF SOMEONE SAYS, "ALL GODS ARE THE SAME"?

The only true God is the Creator (Acts 17:24). Other gods were made by human hands and minds, but the triune God made us, carries us, and saves us (Isaiah 46:3–7).

‖ II. GOD IS OUR FATHER

Read Luke 15:11–24.

A. What things did the younger son do to his father? How do you imagine the father felt?

By asking for his share of the inheritance, the son effectively wished his father dead. He disrespected and abandoned him, abusing his father's generosity and love. He wasted his father's possessions (rather than using them to care for the family and estate) and disgraced his father in the eyes of others. The father must have been heartbroken as well as humiliated and disappointed.

B. How did the father show unconditional love for the son? What is astonishing about the father's actions?

He watched and waited for his son to return (how else could he have noticed him coming from "a long way off"?). He held up his robes and ran to his son in a completely undignified way. He not only welcomed him back but he also reinstated him and gave him even greater riches than he had before! The father took on the son's disgrace as his own and took the risk of blessing his son again, not knowing how he would act going forward.

C. How are we like the younger son? How is God like the father?

God has given us everything we have, and we often waste it with no regard for Him. We spend these gifts on our own pleasures and try to stay as far away from God as possible. We disrespect Him and shame His name in the world. And yet, like the father, God waits for us. He welcomes us back. And He showers on us more riches of grace than we could ever deserve!

APPLICATION

In what ways can you see yourself in the older son? How was his view of the father also distorted? Are there some of God's children (our lost siblings!) that He's more eager to welcome back into the family than we are?

We often worry about what's fair and judge those we see as more sinful than ourselves. We act as though our standing with God is the result of our faithfulness to Him rather than His mercy to us in Jesus Christ. The older son also didn't really know his father's love. He was more concerned with a fair reward for his labor than a loving relationship with the father. He had the joy of dwelling with the father in his unconditional love, and yet he complained about the lack of a celebratory goat. The father says that everything he has belongs to the son (a position of total abundance), and yet the son lives with a scarcity mindset, clinging tightly to what he believes is owed to him.

Perhaps it's those who've committed overt sexual sins, perhaps the rich (or the poor), perhaps those of a different political party, perhaps people who've hurt us in the past or who have rejected our witness previously—whoever it is, we all have people whose salvation is much less important to us than it is to our Father. If each unbeliever in the world is a brother or sister who's been lost from the family, how could we not most eagerly seek their return?

DIGGING DEEPER

Forgiveness is not free. What did it cost the father to forgive his son? What do you think the father might have suffered for him? What does it cost us to forgive others? What did it cost Jesus to forgive us?

The father certainly lost out monetarily by giving his son additional riches (probably a piece of the other son's inheritance!). He lost dignity by running out to meet his son and probably lost his reputation by accepting back such a disgraceful child. He suffered heartache and grief and relinquished the right to punish the son for his wrongdoing.

It costs us when we forgive others. Forgiving means giving up the right to anger, bitterness, or revenge. It means sacrificing whatever has been lost to us by the other person's sin. To forgive a debt means we absorb the cost of the money that wasn't returned to us. To forgive someone's sin means we absorb the results of that person's action rather than punish him or her in return.

Infinitely greater, however, than any sacrifice we might make to forgive another person is the sacrifice of Jesus. It cost Jesus His life to forgive us! All the debt of sin owed by all the world was absorbed by God when Jesus gave His sinless life on the cross. Jesus has bought a costly forgiveness for you and me, and it is this abundant grace that makes possible our forgiveness of others. It is also because we have been forgiven much that we are commanded to forgive others. This is the point of Jesus' parable of the debtors in Matthew 18:21–35.

APPLICATION

If God is our Father, how does that change how we relate to one another?

Christian faith is not just "me and Jesus." We have a family relationship with other believers, as strong a tie of loyalty and love as if they were blood brothers and sisters. Even unbelievers are lost siblings whom we should be as eager to have back into the family as God is. This also means we have an eternal family that transcends our own flawed human families.

⁞ PRAYER PROMPT

Father God, show us our sin. Reveal the things we have thought, said, and done that are not pleasing to You. Forgive us for our disloyalty and the pain we've caused You, but also for our unforgiveness and unwillingness to welcome back lost siblings.

(Allow time for silent confession.)

PRAY TOGETHER

"Have mercy on me, O God, according to Your steadfast love; according to Your abundant mercy blot out my transgressions. . . . Purge me with hyssop, and I shall be clean; wash me, and I shall be whiter than snow. . . . Create in me a clean heart, O God, and renew a right spirit within me. . . . Restore to me the joy of Your salvation, and uphold me with a willing spirit." (PSALM 51:1, 7, 10, 12)

⁞ HYMN

Sing the hymn on page 32 together.

As time allows, review the essay "Reading the Prodigal Son in Asia" on page 34, or encourage participants to read the essay on their own outside of class.

ARTICLE 2:
NAMES AND TITLES OF JESUS

■ ■ ■

". . . And in Jesus Christ, His only Son, our Lord . . ."

:■ CATECHISM REFERENCE

You shall not misuse the name of the LORD your God.

What does this mean? We should fear and love God so that we do not curse, swear, use satanic arts, lie, or deceive by His name, but call upon it in every trouble, pray, praise, and give thanks.[20]

:■ LESSON OBJECTIVES

By God's grace, we will

- understand from Scripture the meaning of various names and titles of Jesus;

- analyze the connections between these names and titles and Jesus' nature and actions; and

- take comfort in these names and titles as we connect them through prayer to moments and experiences in our own lives.

OPENING PRAYER

Jesus, Your name is above all names. As we look forward to the day when every knee will bow before You, we pray that today our knees and hearts would bow at Your feet and our tongues confess that You are Lord, to the glory of God the Father. Amen.

INTRODUCTION QUESTION

Pick one name of Jesus you find interesting, comforting, or hard to understand. Explain to your group why you picked it.

This phrase from the Creed gives us four names and titles: Jesus is the Christ, the Son, and our Lord. Scripture gives us many, many names, titles, and offices of Jesus! In a small group, look at one of the names or titles and the Bible references in the list that follows, and answer the questions below. Then share your findings with the full group.

▪▪ NAMES AND TITLES OF JESUS QUESTIONS

1. What does this name/title mean?

2. What does this name/title say about who Jesus is?

3. What does this name/title say about what Jesus did/ does?

4. When might you want to pray using this name/title?

5. Draw a picture or think of an image to represent this name/title.

Example: Jesus—Matthew 1:18–21 (Do this one together as a class.)

1. **What does this name/title mean?** *Jesus* means "God saves." The name is *Yeshua* in Hebrew.

    a. *Ye* is from *Yahweh* (styled LORD in most English Bibles), the God of the Bible and the God of the Jews. This was the particular name that God gave Himself in Exodus 3; it is the name by which His people knew Him and identified Him throughout generations. There can be no mistake about whose Son Jesus is or who it is that offers salvation to humanity.

    b. *Shua* is from the Hebrew *Yasha*, which means "to save or deliver."

2. **What does this name/title say about who Jesus is?** Jesus is from God and is God. He was sent by the historical God of the Bible, from the same line of faith as the Old Testament Jewish people. Jesus' identity is the salvation that comes from God.

3. **What does this name/title say about what Jesus did/does?** This is perhaps the clearest, most central statement of what Jesus did. Jesus came to earth to save us from sin. He fulfilled the promises of salvation that Yahweh had given His people since the fall into sin.

4. **When might you want to pray using this name/title?** We might start a prayer of confession by saying, "Dear Jesus, please forgive me for . . ." Or in a time of feeling distant from God, we might pray using the name Jesus, knowing He is from God and of God, the one who brings us back to the Father.

5. **Draw a picture or think of an image to represent this name/title.** For an image, write out *Jesus* so that the middle S is tall and the name forms a cross.

NAMES AND TITLES OF JESUS

A. *Immanuel—Matthew 1:18–23; John 14:9–11*

1. **What does this name/title mean?** "God with us."

2. **What does this name/title say about who Jesus is?** This tells us that Jesus is fully God (not just *from* God). He dwells among us with His eternal presence. He and the Father are one.

3. **What does this name/title say about what Jesus did/does?** Jesus is God come to earth so we could know Him. He came to speak the words and do the works of the Father. He is the promised Savior, the fulfillment of Isaiah's prophecy.

4. **When might you want to pray using this name/title?** We might pray to Immanuel in a time of feeling lonely or forgotten.

5. **Draw a picture or think of an image to represent this name/title.** Allow participants to use their imagination.

B. Christ/Messiah—John 1:40–42; John 4:25–26; John 20:30–31

1. **What does this name/title mean?** "Anointed one" or "chosen Savior." In Jesus' Baptism, God the Father anointed Jesus with the Holy Spirit.

2. **What does this name/title say about who Jesus is?** Jesus is the answer to all the Old Testament promises, the one the Jewish people had been waiting for.

3. **What does this name/title say about what Jesus did/does?** Jesus explains things, making known to people the mystery of salvation. He saves. He did all of the miraculous works the Messiah was prophesied to do, and He offers eternal life to all who believe in Him.

4. **When might you want to pray using this name/title?** We might use the title Christ when praying for salvation, remembering and praising God for His fulfilled promises, or praying for a promise not yet fulfilled.

5. **Draw a picture or think of an image to represent this name/title.** Allow participants to use their imagination.

Note A: Christ is Greek and *Messiah* is Hebrew, but they both have the same meaning: "anointed one." This was the title the Jews used for the promised Savior, the special, chosen leader that God would send to save both the Jews and the whole world.

C. The Word—John 1:1–3, 14 (read the verses again, substituting "Jesus" every time you see "Word" or "He"); Psalm 33:6

1. **What does this name/title mean?** Jesus is the Word from God, the power of creation and salvation, the power of Scripture.

2. **What does this name/title say about who Jesus is?** Jesus is what God's Word is—true, efficacious, powerful, glorious, gracious. He is fully God from eternity.

3. **What does this name/title say about what Jesus did/does?** God created everything through His spoken word. Jesus is the source of creation and was actively involved in the making of the world. He came to live among us as God with flesh on.

4. **When might you want to pray using this name/title?** We might use this name in praying for faith or understanding. Before reading Scripture, we might pray for the Word to open to us the Bible's meaning and its power.

5. **Draw a picture or think of an image to represent this name/title.** Allow participants to use their imagination.

D. *Son of God—Mark 1:1, 9–11; John 5:17–23*

1. **What does this name/title mean?** "Begotten of God."

2. **What does this name/title say about who Jesus is?** As the Son of God, Jesus is equal with God the Father and worthy of honor.

3. **What does this name/title say about what Jesus did/does?** Jesus pleased and obeyed the Father in everything. He fully did God's will and glorified Him with His life. Jesus makes God known to us and brings us by Baptism to be His brothers and sisters, children of God.

4. **When might you want to pray using this name/title?** We might use this title in praying for closeness with God or praying to live a life pleasing to the Father.

5. **Draw a picture or think of an image to represent this name/title.** Allow participants to use their imagination.

Review John 5:17–23. Does this mean Jesus is not God?
No. It is clear from this passage that the title "Son of God" makes Jesus equal with God, equally worthy of honor, equal in action. People who try to say that Jesus never claimed to be God completely miss the reason the Jewish leaders called for His execution!

E. Son of Man—Daniel 7:13–14; Mark 10:43–45; Matthew 26:63–65

1. **What does this name/title mean?** The meaning of this name has two senses. It marks Jesus as human like us, but it also marks Him as a glorious fulfillment of prophecy, holy and worthy of worship.

2. **What does this name/title say about who Jesus is?** Jesus is God and He is human. He fulfilled God's prophecies to Daniel.

3. **What does this name/title say about what Jesus did/does?** He is King. God has made Him ruler over an eternal kingdom that includes people from all the earth. He is seated in power in heaven. And yet, Jesus also came to serve and to give Himself up for us.

4. **When might you want to pray using this name/title?** We might use this name when we feel burdened by life and want to remember that Jesus (a son of man) understands. Or we might use this name to praise Jesus for His glory.

5. **Draw a picture or think of an image to represent this name/title.** Allow participants to use their imagination.

Note B: "Son of Man" (Jesus' most common way of referencing Himself) carries a double meaning. It is a way of emphasizing His humanity, contrasting with the name Son of God. However, this name is also a powerful Old Testament reference to Daniel 7. Jesus claimed to be the "one like a son of man" (Daniel 7:13), holy and worthy of worship, whom Daniel saw in heaven. This claim is what so greatly upset the high priest.

F. Lord—Romans 10:9–13; Philippians 2:9–11

1. **What does this name/title mean?** "Master, ruler, authority."

2. **What does this name/title say about who Jesus is?** Jesus is ruler over all people and has all power. He deserves our submission and obedience. All creation and every spiritual power bows before Him.

3. **What does this name/title say about what Jesus did/does?** He saves those who call on Him, rules over our lives, and reigns over heaven and earth. He saves us from ever being put to shame. Because He is the all-powerful ruler over creation and we belong to Him, Satan could never shame us with his lies, nor can any earthly failure or the judgments of others cause us true shame.

4. **When might you want to pray using this name/title?** We might call on the Lord in praying for Jesus' power or praying for us to have the humility to submit to and follow Him. In a time of experiencing earthly shame, we can call on the Lord, who gives true honor.

5. **Draw a picture or think of an image to represent this name/title.** Allow participants to use their imagination.

G. Lamb of God—John 1:29–31; Hebrews 10:1–10

1. **What does this name/title mean?** Jesus was the perfect sacrifice for sin, the sacrifice that God provided.

2. **What does this name/title say about who Jesus is?** Jesus is perfect and holy (without blemish). He is our substitute, the sacrifice for our sins.

3. **What does this name/title say about what Jesus did/does?**
    He gave Himself up to forgive our sins and those of the whole
    world. We have been declared holy because He has done God's
    will and sacrificed Himself for us. He fulfilled the sacrificial
    system once and for all by offering a lasting solution for sin.
4. **When might you want to pray using this name/title?** We
    might pray to Jesus as the Lamb of God when remembering
    His sacrifice for us or when praying for forgiveness from our
    sins.
5. **Draw a picture or think of an image to represent this name/
    title.** Allow participants to use their imagination.

H. *Light of the World—John 8:12; Matthew 4:12–17*

1. **What does this name/title mean?** Truth, guide, revealer, life,
    opposite of darkness (which represents sin, confusion, lost-
    ness, death).
2. **What does this name/title say about who Jesus is?** Jesus
    is true, illuminating, life-giving, and righteous.
3. **What does this name/title say about what Jesus did/does?**
    He gives life, shows the way for us to live, and scatters the
    darkness of sin and death in the world.
4. **When might you want to pray using this name/title?** We
    might pray to Jesus as Light when praying for God's work in
    the world, for more people to be saved, for a greater under-
    standing of the truth, for guidance in life, in a time of darkness
    and confusion, or in the midst of suffering.
5. **Draw a picture or think of an image to represent this name/
    title.** Allow participants to use their imagination.

I. The Resurrection and the Life—John 11:23–27; 1 Corinthians 15:20–23

1. **What does this name/title mean?** Life after death, eternal life, source of true and full life now and forever.

2. **What does this name/title say about who Jesus is?** Jesus is life. The resurrection is not an idea or a theology; it's a person! Jesus is the firstfruits—the guarantee of the final resurrection.

3. **What does this name/title say about what Jesus did/does?** He raised the dead and Himself rose again. He gives us life after death and eternal life starting now for all those who believe in Him. He defeated death and its hold on people.

4. **When might you want to pray using this name/title?** We might use this name in praying for the family of believers who have died or when praying for someone who is sick. When we feel like life is futile or we face the reality of how brief our earthly lives truly are, we can take comfort in Jesus, the Resurrection.

5. **Draw a picture or think of an image to represent this name/title.** Allow participants to use their imagination.

J. Prophet—Deuteronomy 18:15–19; Acts 3:19–23; Luke 7:14–16; Matthew 24:3–14

1. **What does this name/title mean?** Someone who speaks God's words, tells the future, performs miracles.

2. **What does this name/title say about who Jesus is?** Jesus is the greatest of all the prophets; He is the fulfillment of all the Old Testament prophets and God's promise for a great prophet to come.

3. **What does this name/title say about what Jesus did/does?** Jesus spoke God's Word in truth and fullness, so all people

must listen to Him. Jesus did miracles. Jesus prophesied about the end of the world and what to expect before He returns.

4. **When might you want to pray using this name/title?** We might pray to Jesus as prophet when we want to know the truth or are looking for guidance. We might also pray to the Prophet in times of uncertainty about the future, looking to Him who knows all that is to come.

5. **Draw a picture or think of an image to represent this name/ title.** Allow participants to use their imagination.

Note C: Prophets in the Old Testament had three jobs:

1. Speak God's words to people

2. Prophesy

3. Perform healings and miracles

K. Priest—Hebrews 7:23–27; Hebrews 4:14–16

1. **What does this name/title mean?** Someone who goes between people and God.

2. **What does this name/title say about who Jesus is?** Jesus is the perfect mediator. He is holy and set apart, with no sins of His own to atone for. And yet He knows and understands us completely.

3. **What does this name/title say about what Jesus did/does?** Jesus gave the perfect sacrifice and gives us access to God's throne, where we can always find mercy and grace. He intercedes eternally for us and for our salvation.

4. **When might you want to pray using this name/title?** We might pray to Jesus the High Priest when asking for

forgiveness. We could also use the title Priest when bringing requests before God, remembering that only through Jesus can we have access to God's throne.

5. **Draw a picture or think of an image to represent this name/ title.** Allow participants to use their imagination.

L. *King/King of kings—Revelation 1:4–5; John 18:33–37*

1. **What does this name/title mean?** Ruler over everything.

2. **What does this name/title say about who Jesus is?** Jesus is greater than any human king or ruler. He is the ruler of a heavenly kingdom. Jesus has all the power and glory.

3. **What does this name/title say about what Jesus did/does?** Jesus reigns from heaven over all of His creation, all of heaven and earth, things seen and unseen. He is king over every ruler and authority. Someday He will return in glory and reign fully and visibly over the new heaven and new earth.

4. **When might you want to pray using this name/title?** We might use this title in praying to Jesus in His power and praising Him for His glorious greatness. We might pray to Jesus the King on behalf of human rulers, asking Him to guide and rule over them. And we pray to King Jesus when we ask for His kingdom to come and His will to be done.

5. **Draw a picture or think of an image to represent this name/ title.** Allow participants to use their imagination.

Putting it all together, what have we learned about who Jesus is and what He did then and does for us now? Take notes as others share their findings.

WHO JESUS IS	WHAT JESUS DID/DOES

**So that at the name of Jesus every knee should bow,
in heaven and on earth and under the earth.**

(PHILIPPIANS 2:10)

PRAYER PROMPTS

• *Thank God for sending Jesus, and praise Jesus for who He is.*
• *Pray for grace to know Jesus more.*
• *Pray requests based on the name or title of Jesus that you studied.*

CLOSING

Sing the hymn on page 48 together.

As time allows, review the essay "Prayer: Foreign or Familiar?" on page 50, or encourage participants to read the essay on their own outside of class.

ARTICLE 2:
WHY DID JESUS COME?

■ ■ ■

". . . And in Jesus Christ, His
only Son, our Lord . . ."

▪▪ CATECHISM REFERENCE

And in Jesus Christ, His only Son, our Lord, who was conceived by the Holy Spirit, born of the Virgin Mary, suffered under Pontius Pilate, was crucified, died and was buried. He descended into hell. The third day He rose again from the dead. He ascended into heaven and sits at the right hand of God, the Father Almighty. From thence He will come to judge the living and the dead.

What does this mean? I believe that Jesus Christ, true God, begotten of the Father from eternity, and also true man, born of the Virgin Mary, is my Lord, who has redeemed me, a lost and condemned person, purchased and won me from all sins, from death, and from the power of the devil; not with gold or silver, but with His holy, precious blood and with His innocent suffering and death, that I may be His own and live under Him in His kingdom and serve Him in everlasting righteousness, innocence, and blessedness, just as He is risen from the dead, lives and reigns to all eternity. This is most certainly true.[21]

ⵄ LESSON OBJECTIVES

By God's grace, we will

- articulate from Scripture how it is that people can know God;

- rest in the assurance that God wants us to know Him and sent Jesus so that we can have this knowledge and relationship; and

- consider the fundamentally relational nature of redemption and salvation through Jesus Christ.

ⵄ OPENING PRAYER

Christ, precious Word of God, You promised to dwell among us always. Give to us Your light that we might know the Father and be reconciled to Him. Amen.

ⵄ INTRODUCTION QUESTION

If you could eat dinner with any one person (past or present), who would you want to eat with? Why?

▐▪ OPENING DISCUSSION

We might take the answers to the following questions for granted, but much of the world doesn't. Consider carefully how you would respond and explain the answers to someone else.

• *Can I know God? How?*

• *Does God want to know me? Why?*

Let students discuss openly. Don't try to direct conversation unless it's just to add a question to help them think through these questions more deeply. Allow students to wrestle and perhaps be a bit uncomfortable.

▐▪ REASON 1: JESUS CAME SO WE COULD KNOW GOD.

Read John 1:14–18.

How can we know God?

Verse 18 makes clear that no one has seen God. We see evidence of God's glory and divine power in creation (Romans 1:20), but creation itself has been broken by sin. Seeing God's created works gives us only partial knowledge of who He is (for example, it tells us of His power but tells nothing of His grace). Since we can't know God the Father by seeing Him face-to-face, Jesus—the one and only Son—came to make Him known to us. The Law given to Moses (John 1:17) showed God's character and His righteous judgment, allowing people to know God in part. The Old Testament Scriptures spoke of the promised Messiah and the hope of God's gracious deliverance. In Jesus, God's grace and truth were fully revealed for all humanity. From Christ, we receive "grace upon grace" (John 1:16)—an infinite store of grace and mercy.

What do these verses show about God's desire to know us and be known by us?

It's a deep desire! When God made us in His image (Genesis 1:27), He made us to be relational and to be complete only when we are in relationship with Him. As God graciously sought out Adam and Eve after they sinned, calling out "Where are you?" (Genesis 3:9) as a merciful invitation to come back to Him and be known by Him, so He continues to seek all people. He was willing to send His Son, willing to take on flesh and dwell with us, so that we could know Him. His purpose in sending Jesus was to make Himself known. "For now we see in a mirror dimly, but then face to face. Now I know in part; then I shall know fully, even as I have been fully known" (1 Corinthians 13:12).

APPLICATION

What does this mean about the value of people? this world? you?

Since Jesus, the Son of God, became man and came to live on earth, it means God's world is important to Him! God was and is working here in this physical world. Jesus "became flesh and dwelt among us" (John 1:14). The people God created are important to Him. Jesus cared to dwell among people and reveal His glory to them—and this includes you and each person with whom you come into contact. And the promise of the new heaven and new earth (Revelation 21:1; 2 Peter 3:13; Isaiah 65:17; Isaiah 66:22) is an even greater fulfillment of this—not just that Jesus will take on flesh in one place and time, but that in eternity "the dwelling place of God is with man. He will dwell with them, and they will be His people, and God Himself will be with them as their God" (Revelation 21:3).

Read John 14:5–14.

How does Jesus describe the relationship between Him and His Father?

If we know Jesus, we know God the Father. When the disciples saw Jesus, they saw God. Jesus and His Father are distinct and yet perfectly one.

According to these verses, why is faith in Jesus necessary?

Simply put, Jesus is the only way to the Father. He is the way to life, salvation, and an eternity of dwelling with God. Jesus was our substitute, living in our place the perfect life God demands if we are to live in His presence, and suffering in our place, completely satisfying God's wrath at our sins on the cross. He is the Truth, the Word of God made flesh so we can know God and know what is true. He is the Life, the source of the resurrection and of everlasting life.

DIGGING DEEPER

John 14:13–14 can be easily misunderstood to suggest "in Jesus' name, amen" is a magical formula for making sure our prayers are answered as we wish them to be. What does it really mean to pray "in Jesus' name?" (Consider: What would it mean to give a donation in someone else's name or sign a document in another person's name?)

To do something in someone's name means with that person's authority and will. Jesus, who has all authority in heaven and on earth (Matthew 28:18), invites us to pray in His name and ask boldly from the Father (John 16:23–24). Because Christ is our High Priest, we can approach God's throne with confidence (Hebrews 4:16). When we pray using the phrase "in Jesus' name," we are praying for God to work by His authority whatever is in accord with His will.

What does Jesus say is the end goal of doing for us what we ask in His name (John 14:13)?

The goal is God's glory. When God answers our prayers for the sake of Jesus, He proves how trustworthy, loving, and gracious He is. That makes us more confident to pray to Him, and it gives us the chance to glorify God as we tell others the great things He has done. But selfish prayers, ungodly desires, or prayers that are not the will of God cannot bring glory to God. Such prayers deny God's authority and seek only our own will, turning our act of prayer into one of idolatry (sin against the First Commandment) rather than worship of God. Praise God that in His mercy He does not grant such prayers! Jesus does promise that prayer carries power, but the power and the will are His, not ours.

⠿ REASON 2: HE CAME TO SAVE US FROM SIN.

> **For there is no distinction: for all have sinned and fall short of the glory of God.** (ROMANS 3:22–23)
>
> **For the wages of sin is death.** (ROMANS 6:23)

We were created to be in relationship with God. Relationship with God is life. Sin separates us from God and thus sin leads to death. God is just—but He loves us. He must punish sin—but He doesn't want us to die eternally. We need a substitute.

> **For Christ also suffered once for sins, the righteous for the unrighteous, that He might bring us to God.**
>
> (1 PETER 3:18)

Christ is the substitute we need! He is the righteous one who kept God's Law and glorified the Father perfectly, and yet He willingly took upon Himself our unrighteousness, our separation from God, the death our sins deserved. In Christ, God maintained His honor and justice by upholding the Law, and yet He demonstrated His great love and mercy, making a way for us sinners to be reconciled to Him.

How does 1 Peter 3:18 describe the result of our salvation? In what way is this the same and different from saying, "You must believe in Jesus so you don't go to hell"?

The phrase "that He might bring us to God" certainly includes eternal life with God and excludes the punishment of hell because Jesus took that punishment upon Himself when He carried the sins of the world to the cross. But it doesn't end there. Salvation doesn't only mean a get-out-of-jail-free card. It's about a relationship with God, a relationship that starts right now and that continues eternally.

Read Romans 1:1–4.

Why did Jesus need to be both man and God in order to die to save us?

Because God is eternal, the Son of God had to become human to be able to die in our place. The punishment for sin is death, and someone needed to take this punishment, but any mere human—even a perfect one (if such a person existed)—could not save the world by his death. Only the Son of God made man could do that.

What is the greatest proof of Jesus' divinity (v. 4)?

Jesus' resurrection is the fullest proof of His divinity. Only God can raise the dead. Jesus was active with His Father and the Holy Spirit in His own resurrection, conquering death by raising Himself from the grave (John 2:19). Jesus also proved His divinity by raising others from the dead (see Lazarus, John 11:1–44; Jairus's daughter, Mark 5:21–43), by controlling nature (see calming the storm, Mark 4:35–41), and at His transfiguration (Matthew 17:1–9).

> **For God so loved the world, that he gave His only Son, that whoever believes in Him should not perish but have eternal life.** (JOHN 3:16)

What was God's motive for saving us?

God loved the world He created and loved us individually as His beloved children.

Who receives salvation and eternal life?[22]

Whoever believes in Jesus has eternal life! Or as Mark 16:16 tells us, "Whoever believes and is baptized will be saved."

*This is the most basic tenet of Christianity and one we know well, but how would you explain to someone what it means to **believe** in Jesus? What exactly do we have to believe about Him? How much does someone have to know to be saved? What other words could we use to explain* **believe***?*

Spend significant time on this question because it's important for Christians to be able to articulate. Think about what the Apostles' Creed considers essential to know and believe about Jesus (see Jesus' incarnation, His divinity, His suffering and death in our place, His resurrection, the forgiveness of sins, and eternal salvation imparted to us through Christ, and such things).

The Athanasian Creed puts it this way: "It is also necessary for everlasting salvation that one faithfully believe the incarnation of our Lord Jesus Christ. Therefore, it is the right faith that we believe and confess that our Lord Jesus Christ, the Son of God, is at the same time both God and Man." (*LSB*, pages 319–20, paragraphs 27–28).

Consider other words, like *trust* and *rely*. To believe is not just to know or say things but to trust in Christ and rely on God for our salvation. We are not saved by our knowledge or theological understanding; if we imply that we are, we put the weight of salvation back upon the shoulders of the believer.

APPLICATION

Speak the Gospel to the person next to you by reading this paraphrase of John 3:16 and putting his or her name in each blank. Rejoice in this wonderful truth!

For God so loved .... that He gave His one and only Son, that if .... believes in Him, ... will not perish but ....
will have eternal life.

Look at the Second Article of the Creed, which summarizes who Jesus is (names and titles, His divinity and humanity) and what He did to save us (His suffering, death, resurrection, and ascension).

> And in Jesus Christ, His only Son, our Lord,
>
> who was conceived by the Holy Spirit,
>
> born of the Virgin Mary,
>
> suffered under Pontius Pilate,
>
> was crucified, died and was buried.
>
> He descended into hell.
>
> The third day He rose again from the dead.
>
> He ascended into heaven
>
> and sits at the right hand of God, the Father Almighty.
>
> From thence He will come to judge the living and the dead.

Below are some common misunderstandings about Jesus.[23] Answer each misconception, using one or more Bible verses from this lesson or by referencing other Bible passages. Consider also which phrase from the Creed you would use to answer these statements.

Additional texts are provided in parentheses for leader reference. If students have questions or confusion or want to learn more about any of these topics, you can lead them through these passages. However, the focus of this discussion is to allow students to apply the things they have studied in this lesson to conversations they might have with other people. Don't feel a need to read aloud all the supplemental passages.

1. Jesus was only a good teacher. He wasn't God.

John 1:14: Jesus was present at creation; He became man and God's glory dwelt with Him. Romans 1:4: Jesus' resurrection proves His divinity. From the Creed: "conceived by the Holy Spirit," "sits at the right hand of God." (See also John 20:28; John 10:30; Romans 9:5; 1 John 5:20.)

2. God could never understand our human life and experience.

John 1:14: Jesus took on flesh and came to dwell among us as a man. From the Creed: "born of the virgin Mary," "suffered . . . crucified, died." Answers should also include illustrations from Jesus' life on earth that are specific to His humanity. (See also 2 Corinthians 8:9; Isaiah 53:3; Philippians 2:5–8; Hebrews 2:14–18.)

3. God is too great and distant for humans to ever know conclusively who He is or what He is like.

John 1:18: Jesus made God known to us. From the Creed: "His only Son, our Lord," "born of the virgin Mary," "He is at the right hand of God" [intercedes for us]. From Lesson 2, He is called *Immanuel*, which means "God with us." (See also John 20:31; Colossians 1:15–20; Hebrews 1:1–2; Romans 8:34.)

4. There is no way God could ever accept me.

John 1:16: From Jesus we have received grace upon grace. John 14:6: God can and does accept believers through His Son, Jesus. 1 Peter 3:18: Christ suffered to bring us to God. John 3:16: Those who believe in Jesus have eternal life. (See also Acts 4:12; Romans 8:31–34; Romans 5:1–2; John 6:37–40.)

5. All faiths are the same. There are many ways to find God.

John 14:6: No one comes to the Father except through His Son, Jesus. From the Creed: "I believe in Jesus Christ, His *only* Son, our Lord" (emphasis added). (See also Deuteronomy 6:4; 1 Corinthians 8:4–6; Isaiah 42:8; Matthew 4:10.)

:• PRAYER PROMPT

Pray in partners, using the words of Ephesians 3:16–19 and putting the other person's name in the blank.

I pray that out of God's great riches He may strengthen .... with power through His Spirit in .... 's inner being, so that Christ may dwell in .... 's heart through faith.

And I pray that .... would be rooted and built up in love.

I pray that .... may have power, together with all Christians, to know how wide and long and high and deep is the love of Christ.

And I pray that .... may know this love that is beyond knowing—so that .... may be filled with all the fullness of God.

▪ HYMN

▪ CLOSING

Sing the hymn on page 63 together.

As time allows, review the essay "To Know and Be Known" on page 64, or encourage participants to read the essay on their own outside of class.

ARTICLE 3:
I BELIEVE
IN THE HOLY SPIRIT
■ ■ ■

"I believe in the Holy Spirit, the holy Christian church, the communion of saints, the forgiveness of sins, the resurrection of the body, and the life everlasting. Amen."

▪▪ CATECHISM REFERENCE

What does this mean? I believe that I cannot by my own reason or strength believe in Jesus Christ, my Lord, or come to Him; but the Holy Spirit has called me by the Gospel, enlightened me with His gifts, sanctified and kept me in the true faith. In the same way He calls, gathers, enlightens, and sanctifies the whole Christian church on earth, and keeps it with Jesus Christ in the one true faith.[24]

▪▪ LESSON OBJECTIVES

By God's grace, we will

- articulate from Scripture who the Holy Spirit is and what He does;

- take comfort in knowing how we can recognize the Holy Spirit's presence and work; and

- be humbled in recognizing all that we cannot understand or control about the Holy Spirit.

▪▪ OPENING PRAYER

Holy Spirit, divine helper, teach us all things and bring to our remembrance all that Jesus said and did. Dwell in us always and lead us into all truth. In Jesus' name. Amen.

▪▪ INTRODUCTION QUESTION

If you could choose one of these superpowers, which would you choose?

• *Be able to speak any language*

• *Be able to travel instantly from one place to another*

• *Be able to know what other people are thinking*

These are, of course, all things the Holy Spirit can do as the Third Person of the Trinity and things He has at times enabled people in the Bible to do.

▪▪ KEY QUESTIONS

Although this lesson is much more teacher centered than any of the others (primarily because this is a subject about which there is much confusion among both new and longtime believers), these questions will keep the focus on student thought and application. Make sure to leave significant time for their discussion at the end of the lesson.

1. Why do we need the Holy Spirit?

2. How can I know if I have God's Spirit living in me?

3. How can I make someone else believe in Jesus?

Rather than being open discussion questions, these are simply a guiding framework for the lesson. By the end of the lesson, students should be able to confidently answer these questions. For now, just pose the questions and ask students to keep them in mind throughout the lesson.

▪▪ I. WHO IS THE HOLY SPIRIT?

A. The Holy Spirit is the Third Person of the Trinity: Father, Son and Holy Spirit.

B. The Bible describes specific roles the Holy Spirit has, but the triune God is always united in these works. The Nicene Creed reminds us that the Holy Spirit proceeds from (is sent

by) the Father and the Son—the Trinity working in unity for our salvation.

1. The Holy Spirit's character is the same as God's character. Think of one example. God is ....

There are many possible answers: holy, loving, just, omnipotent, eternal, etc.

2. The Holy Spirit's will is the same as God's will. Think of one example. God's will is ....

In brief, God's will is for all people to be saved (1 Timothy 2:4) and for us to live sanctified lives (1 Thessalonians 4:3). We can get into long discussions about seeking God's will for our individual lives and daily decisions, but most Scripture references about God's will are very clear—His will is to reconcile people to Himself.

3. The Holy Spirit's work is the same as God's work. Think of one example. God is working in the world to ....

There are many answers: seek and save the lost, equip believers, provide for people's needs, sustain creation, etc.

▪▪ II. WHAT HAS THE HOLY SPIRIT DONE IN THE PAST?

A. Read Genesis 1:1–3. At the beginning, the Holy Spirit

was active in God's work of creating the heavens and earth.

B. Read 2 Peter 1:20–21. Throughout the Bible, the Holy Spirit

inspired the writers of Scripture.

C. Read Luke 1:35. Before Jesus' birth, the Holy Spirit

brought about His incarnation.

D. Read Matthew 3:13–17. At Jesus' Baptism, the Holy Spirit

came in the form of a dove, testifying with the Father to who Jesus is and dwelling with Jesus.

E. Read Luke 4:1, 14. During Jesus' ministry, the Holy Spirit

was with Jesus, giving Him power and leading Him.

F. Read Acts 2:1–11. After Jesus returned to heaven, the Holy Spirit

was poured out on the apostles, empowering them to declare the Gospel in many languages and bringing many people to faith.

G. Read Psalm 143:10; Psalm 51:10–11; and Psalm 139:7. Was the Holy Spirit present in the world and in believers before Pentecost?

Yes, the Spirit has always been in the world—creating and preserving faith, leading believers, forgiving them, being present with them, and so forth. At Pentecost, the Spirit was poured out in a new, prophecy-fulfilling way, ushering in the last days (Acts 2:17–18).

III. WHAT DOES THE HOLY SPIRIT DO NOW?

Read John 16:7–15. What did Jesus tell His disciples about the sending of the Holy Spirit and the Spirit's work? Why is it to their (and our!) advantage that Jesus is no longer walking on this earth?

Jesus promised that He would send the Holy Spirit when He returned to the Father. The Spirit, or Advocate, guides Jesus' followers into truth—helping us understand God's Word and Christ's work of redemption through the cross and empty tomb. He convicts the world by God's Law, showing us our sin and how we have fallen short of God's righteousness. His work is to glorify Jesus and to help us understand what God has spoken to us in His Word.

Astonishingly, Jesus says that it is to His disciples' advantage that He go back to the Father! We might feel at a disadvantage because we don't have Jesus' physical presence with us, but His physical body (pre-resurrection) was bound by space and time. The Spirit dwells with each believer at all times and in all spaces. It was to the disciples' advantage for Jesus to go away because He "went away" in order to die, rise, and ascend for our salvation. Jesus taught His disciples many things, but the Spirit now works within us, guiding us to understand, believe, and apply these truths.

A. If you are a believer, some of the Spirit's work is **already done!** *Only by the Holy Spirit's work through the Word and Sacraments can we say,* "Jesus is Lord" *(1 Corinthians 12:3).*

B. If you are a believer, some of this work is **still being done.**

> **But the fruit of the Spirit is love, joy, peace, patience, kindness, goodness, faithfulness, gentleness, self-control; against such things there is no law. And those who belong to Christ Jesus have crucified the flesh with its passions and desires. If we live by the Spirit, let us also keep in step with the Spirit.**
>
> (GALATIANS 5:22–25)

Why do you think the Bible describes this as *"fruit"*?

This question is rich for discussion, with many possible answers. Fruit is the result of a process; growing fruit takes time. As a healthy tree will always continue to provide fruit in abundance, so the Spirit's gifts never run dry. Fruit benefits the eater and brings joy and praise to the grower; it is not grown for the sake of the tree. Fruit relies on the power of soil, sun, and rain; a tree can't make fruit on its own.

Note also that the Spirit's fruit is singular. A true Spirit-filled life results in all of these things together. It is not enough to be peaceful without faithfulness or self-controlled without love. We may be able to personally manufacture one quality or another based on our natural temperament, but to have all of these qualities in unity can only be the work of the Holy Spirit.

▌▌ IV. HOW DOES THE HOLY SPIRIT COME TO US?

Read Acts 2:38 and Luke 11:13. What answers do these verses give to this question?

The Holy Spirit comes through the Word of God and through Baptism. When Peter and the others preached to the crowds at Pentecost, the Holy Spirit moved them to confess their sin and believe the Gospel. They received forgiveness through the waters of Baptism, and the Spirit came to live in their hearts. So, too, when we are baptized into Christ Jesus, we receive as God's gift to us "a life-giving water, rich in grace, and a washing of the new birth in the Holy Spirit."[25]

Jesus also promises that everyone who asks God for the Spirit will receive Him as a good and gracious gift from the Father, who alone provides all that we need for both body and soul. As Luther says, "Nothing is more necessary in Christendom than continual and unceasing prayer that God would give His grace and His Spirit."[26]

175

▪ KEY POINTS TO REMEMBER

1. We *can't explain everything* about the Spirit or limit how and when He works. He is God. He is free to work how He wants to work (John 3:8).

2. The Holy Spirit is a *gift* from God. We can't tell Him what to do. We can't do anything to deserve Him or His work in us (Galatians 3:2–5, 14).

3. The Spirit always works *through the Word of God*. If you want more peace, joy, and confidence in God, read God's Word. If you want to understand more of God's Word, pray for the Spirit's help (John 6:63).

4. The Spirit is always united with the Father and Son. *God is ONE*. Don't try to separate the Trinity. The Spirit is always doing the Father's work and always pointing to Jesus (John 14:26).

APPLICATION

Now go back to the three key questions with which we opened the lesson. Answer these, using what we studied about the Holy Spirit.

1. Why do we need the Holy Spirit?

Only by the Spirit can we have faith in Jesus as our Savior. Only by the Spirit can we grow in sanctification to be more like God.

2. How can I know if I have God's Spirit living in me?

If you say Jesus is Lord, you have the Holy Spirit! If you have been baptized into Christ Jesus, claimed by God as His child and washed by water and His Word, you have been given the Holy Spirit.[27] There is much that is mysterious about the Spirit's work, but believers never need to worry about whether or not the Spirit is living in them. This is a certain promise we have from God's Word and the Sacraments.

The fruit of the Spirit is also a manifestation of the Holy Spirit's work in us. Where you see this fruit in yourself and in others, praise God! Where you don't see this fruit in your own life, keep praying for the Spirit to lead you to repentance, give you greater trust in Christ's forgiveness, and fill you with His love, joy, peace, patience, kindness, goodness, faithfulness, gentleness, and self-control. As Jesus promised, God will give the Spirit to all those who ask.

3. How can I make someone else believe in Jesus?

This is included as a trick question—but an important one! You can't. Only God can give faith. Be assured that this is God's action upon us. We receive His Spirit by His work, not by any work we do. (This doesn't mean we are not called to witness to others, but it does mean the burden of the result is on God, not us.) Reference the essay "How Can I Make Them Believe" on page 76.

Christian parents take their children to be baptized because Jesus said to "go therefore and make disciples of all nations, baptizing them in the name of the Father and of the Son and of the Holy Spirit" (Matthew 28:19). This work of God upon us, this visible means of His continuous grace, is done one time, according to Ephesians 4:4–7:

> There is one body and one Spirit—just as you were called to the one hope that belongs to your call—one Lord, one faith, one baptism, one God and Father of all, who is over all and through all and in all.

> **But grace was given to each one of us according to the measure of Christ's gift.**

▪ PRAYER PROMPTS

- *Praise God for the gifts of the Spirit in history and in your life.*
- *Pray for the fruit of the Spirit to overflow in your life and church.*
- *Pray for the Holy Spirit's work in the lives of people you know who don't yet know Jesus.*

▪ CLOSING

Sing the hymn on page 75 together.

As time allows, review the essay "How Can I Make Them Believe?" on page 76, or encourage participants to read the essay on their own outside of class.

ARTICLE 3:
I BELIEVE
IN THE CHURCH

■ ■ ■

" I believe in . . . the holy Christian church, the communion of saints . . ."

■ CATECHISM REFERENCE

202. What is the Church?

It is the body of Christ—that is, all people whom the Spirit, by the Means of Grace, has gathered to Christ in faith throughout the world. . . .

Note: The Creed in its original words speaks of the Church as "catholic" (universal)—that is, existing throughout all time and throughout the world, including people who confess and believe in Jesus Christ from every background ("people and nation,"

Revelation 5:9). Another way to say this is to speak of the "Christian Church."

While the word Church, properly speaking, refers to all those who believe in Christ, it is also used in other ways (such as a building, a congregation, a denomination). The word church is used for such things because confessing Christians are found within them.[28]

:: LESSON OBJECTIVES

By God's grace, we will

- examine three scriptural pictures of the Church and consider what each adds to our understanding of the Church;

- reflect honestly on the flaws and failings of the earthly church and ask for God's forgiveness and restoration; and

- discuss the varied times and ways the church can be the Church.

:: OPENING PRAYER

Lord, we praise You for drawing us near in Christ, making us citizens with the saints and members of Your household. Continue to build Your Church together as a dwelling place for Your Spirit. Amen.

▪ INTRODUCTION QUESTION

Talk briefly about a time you either felt strongly like you belonged or felt strongly like an outsider.

▪ OPENING DISCUSSION

What does church *mean? What about* Church? *(See notes on the last page of this lesson as well as the catechism reference above.)*

Help students understand the many different ways this word is used in modern English. It's helpful to recognize that we go to a church and belong to a specific congregation, are part of a church body, and are part of the Church universal. All of these senses of *church/Church* are true and important parts of Christian life. But it's important to distinguish that when we talk about believing in the "holy Christian church" we are talking about more than our individual congregation or denomination. The Church is "all those who believe in Christ."

▪ I. CHURCH = A BUILDING MADE OF PEOPLE

*Key truth: God lives with and in His Church.

Read Ephesians 2:11–22.

A. Verses 19–22 compare believers to what three things? What benefit comes from each?

Christians are	What benefit(s) does this give us?
1. citizens with the saints	Citizens have rights and protections and rulers who provide and care for them. We are part of the covenant people of God along with all those who have been made holy by Christ (the saints).
2. members of the household of God	Family is a strong bond. We have a relationship with a loving, perfect Father and many brothers and sisters who care for us. We live under the protection and provision of the Head of the household (God).
3. a holy temple in the Lord/ dwelling place for God	God lives with and in us (the Church). It's important to recognize the plural "you" in verse 22. Yes, God's Spirit lives in each baptized believer, but here Paul is talking about God's dwelling within the corporate body of the Church. We have His presence with us always.

B. In verses 20–22, Paul describes a building. Draw this building. As you do, think about these questions: What kind of building is it? What's the foundation of the building? Who is included in the building? What's the most important part of the building? Who lives inside this building?

Encourage students to do the actual work of drawing the metaphor Paul describes here to help them visualize these words. The building is a temple; it is created for worship and the presence of God. The foundation is the apostles and prophets—the Scriptures. The most important part, the cornerstone that sets the whole building straight, is Christ. God Himself chooses to dwell here, within the Church.

DIGGING DEEPER

In the Holy Christian Church, we are not divided into Jews and Gentiles. What divisions do we artificially make between ourselves within the body of believers?

There are many possible answers: politics, theological disputes, race/ethnicity, language, family backgrounds, economic status, worship styles. Take time to acknowledge these very real divisions and the power of the cross to unite even the most deeply divided people.

II. CHURCH = THE BODY OF CHRIST

Key truth: God has given each person gifts and united us with Christ as our head. God uses all of us working together with our varied gifts to accomplish His purposes.

Read Romans 12:3–8.

A. What does the image of a body add to our understanding of the Church?

A body has to work together; no part is useful on its own and no part serves its own purposes but only the good of the whole body. Christ, as the head of the body, gives life to each part and directs the purposes of the whole. A body is living and active; the Church is not just made to stand in one place but also to go and do the will of God in the world. A body has many different parts but is in essence only one being. When we consider a human body, we think first of the whole and then the individual parts. Too often, we do the opposite with the Church—thinking of it first as a group of people and then as one entity. In Christ, we are first one Body and then "individually members one of another" (v. 5).

B. *How does this body have both unity and diversity?*

The Body has one head (Christ), one life, and one purpose. All parts belong to one another. And yet, each part is unique with different gifts and a different role to fulfill.

APPLICATION

What gifts has God given you as part of the Body of Christ? It could be something in this list (Romans 12:6–8) or something else. Talk in a group of two or three people and help one another answer.

There are many possible answers. Encourage people to point out the gifts they see in one another. It is often easier to recognize the gifts of others than to see these gifts in ourselves.

III. CHURCH = THE BRIDE OF CHRIST

Key truth: God loves the Church deeply. Jesus makes the Church holy.

Read Ephesians 5:25–33.

A. *How did Jesus make the Church holy?*

Jesus made us holy by giving Himself for us on the cross. He sanctified us through washing and the Word (Baptism). It is His work and His presentation of the Church to the Father that makes us holy in God's sight.

B. What does God see when He looks at the Church? How is this like or unlike what you see when you look at the Church?

God sees the Church "in splendor, without spot or wrinkle or any such thing, . . . holy and without blemish" (v. 27). Think of a young couple in love, how they see each other and talk about each other with love-blind eyes that see only beauty. Even more beautiful is the aged couple who know all of each other's weaknesses and faults intimately and yet still speak of each other with loving words of praise. God is not love-blind to our faults but rather has acted in Christ to make the Church truly holy and without blemish! Sometimes we have glimpses of this—a Baptism, a radically changed life, acts of selfless care for one another in the Church. But often on earth we see a struggling, divided, sinful Church.

C. What does Jesus continue to do for the Church? (See v. 29.) What do you think that means?

Jesus nourishes and cares for the Church through the Word and Sacraments, through the work of pastors and church workers and laypeople caring for one another. This is ongoing work that Jesus promises to continually do for us.

The Church is not made of perfect people, but of people who admit their sin, depend on God's grace, and forgive one another.

- Hard news: This means people in the Church will fail us at times. You will be hurt by others, if you haven't already. The witness of the Church to the world is flawed and broken.

- Good news: This means that even though you are not perfect, you are welcome in God's Church! This also means the power and holiness of the Church is from God—not us. Jesus died to make the Church holy, and His Spirit is working to make her more and more godly!

DIGGING DEEPER

Why do you think we say in the Creed that we believe in "the holy Christian church"? We can see our churches. We can see the worshipers beside us in the pews. Why do we need faith?

The true Church is invisible. When we look at our congregation, our denomination, and even global Christianity, we still see human sinfulness and struggles, and we don't know when we look at others who it is that truly believes. We need faith to see the Church as God intends it and as He sees her though Christ. Only in the new heaven and new earth will we see the perfect, glorified, triumphant Church.

IV. BEING THE CHURCH

Consider: How would you explain what it looks like to be the Church? When do we come together? What do we do when we come together? (Imagine someone asked you not "What do you do at church?" but "What does the Church do?").

The life of the Church is gathered around Word and Sacraments, which strengthen her members to be the Church in their daily lives throughout the week. (Further answers to this question are found in the verses below.)

Therefore, brothers, since we have confidence to enter the holy places by the blood of Jesus, by the new and living way that He opened for us through the curtain, that is, through His flesh, and since we have a great priest over the house of God, let us draw near with a true heart in full assurance of faith, with our hearts sprinkled clean from an evil conscience and our bodies washed with pure water. Let us hold fast the confession of our hope without wavering, for He who promised is faithful. And let us consider how to stir up one another to love and good works, not neglecting to meet together, as is the habit of some, but encouraging one another, and all the more as you see the Day drawing near. (Hebrews 10:19–25)

A. What things do these verses say the Church does together?

Together we have confidence to come to God because of Christ's sacrifice. We have been washed and forgiven in Baptism and given access to the Father through Christ, the Great High Priest. Because of all of this, we stir up one another to love and good works. We encourage one another and hold on to the hope of the Gospel together.

B. What does it look like to stir up other believers to love and good works?

In my experience, this is not something we often do as believers. Note that the Hebrews passage doesn't say to "guilt one other into good works" or "beat one another up for failing to love" but to "stir up one another." Discuss how this can be done in a loving, relational way. (Keep in mind how this follows the description of what we have been given by Christ: confidence before God, assurance of faith, spiritual cleanliness, and such. Knowing we all are starting with these gifts gives us a joyful Gospel motivation for good works.)

C. Why do you think the writer says we must not give up meeting together?

People are often tempted to give up meeting. It is so easy to become busy, distracted, or isolated, but we need the encouragement of fellow saints. The end is coming soon!

> **Let the word of Christ dwell in you richly, teaching and admonishing one another in all wisdom, singing psalms and hymns and spiritual songs, with thankfulness in your hearts to God.** (COLOSSIANS 3:16)

D. What things do these verses say the Church does together?

We teach one another from the Word of Christ that dwells in us. This is not one-directional from pastor to parishioner, although certainly the pastor has a divine call and a responsibility to teach publicly and faithfully. All believers have access to the wisdom of the Word and Spirit and should share the words of Scripture with one another. These verses also call the Church to admonish one another. (Talk about this one! How many of us like doing that? or receiving it?) Finally, it mentions singing with thankfulness! Note that each of these actions is preceded by and filled by the Word of Christ. The Word and Spirit are what make each of these things possible.

And they devoted themselves to the apostles' teaching and the fellowship, to the breaking of bread and the prayers. (ACTS 2:42)

E. What things do these verses say the Church does together?

We study God's Word and listen to faithful teaching. We spend relational time together, eat together (both common meals and sharing of the Sacrament), and pray together. God promises to come to us and work among us by His Word (Isaiah 55:10–11).

DIGGING DEEPER

Of all the activities you listed from these three passages, which ones are done in worship on Sunday? Which might be better done in small groups or one-on-one? (Some might go in more than one place.)

LARGE GROUP	SMALL GROUP	ONE-ON-ONE

Church is not a weekly one-hour activity—it is people who are following Jesus together and living every day for His kingdom and His mission.

APPLICATION

What can we do to be *the Church at times other than Sunday?*

Discuss. Answers will vary.

PRAYER PROMPTS

- *Pray for God's Church to grow here and around the world.*
- *Pray for God to make the Church more united.*
- *Pray for God to help us love the Church and to grant us grace to forgive and heal from hurts that have happened in our churches. Pray also for God to call those who have hurt us to confession and absolution.*
- *Pray for God to show you your gifts and help you use them in the Church.*

NOTES ON CHURCH

1. The word *church* sometimes refers to a building.

2. The word *church* sometimes refers to a group of people who meet regularly in one place to share God's Word and Sacraments and worship Him.

3. The word *Church* (or *the Church*) means "all believers in Jesus in every time and place."

   a. This Church is *invisible.* We don't know who has faith; only God can judge.

b. This Church is *infallible*. Individual churches and denominations may come and go. God's Church will last forever (Matthew 16:16–18).

CLOSING

Sing the hymn on page 91 together.

As time allows, review the essay "Being the Church" on page 94, or encourage participants to read the essay on their own outside of class.

ARTICLE 3:
FOREVER WITH GOD

■ ■ ■

"I believe . . . in the forgiveness of sins, the resurrection of the body, and the life everlasting. Amen."

CATECHISM REFERENCE

204. What is the forgiveness of sins?

God promises that, for Christ's sake, He will not hold our many sins against us.

205. Why does God forgive our sins?

God forgives our sins because He is merciful and because of Christ's atoning sacrifice for all sinners.

223. *What happens to me as a Christian when I die?*

When I die, the God-given unity of my body and spirit will be broken. I will immediately be in the presence of Christ, in heaven, but my body will remain in the grave until the resurrection.

224. *What will happen to me when I am raised from the dead on the Last Day?*

I will enjoy being with Christ in His new creation, in body and soul, forever.

225. *What will happen to this world after we Christians are raised from the dead?*

The present creation, like our own bodies, will be set free from its bondage to corruption, and God will create a new heaven and a new earth.[29]

▪▪ LESSON OBJECTIVES

By God's grace, we will

- understand the trinitarian nature of forgiveness and draw connections between previous lessons and the promise of forgiveness of sins;

- examine the resurrection as the climax of the Creed, Scripture, and our faith lives;

- articulate from Scripture what resurrection and eternal life mean for us now, after death, and at the end of time; and

- marvel at the beauty of what God promises us in eternal life.

▪ OPENING PRAYER

Resurrected and resurrecting Christ, give us faith that we who live and believe in You will never die. Even as You weep with us when we face the deaths of those we love, so also call them forth from their tombs to life everlasting. Amen.

▪ INTRODUCTION QUESTION

Share a Bible verse you want read at your deathbed or funeral. Why did you pick this verse?

Allow time for discussion. Some options are John 3:16; Psalm 23; Matthew 11:28; Romans 6:4; 1 Corinthians 15:54–56; Revelation 21:4.

▪ OPENING DISCUSSION

Why is it important that this phrase in the Creed includes both "the resurrection of the body" and "the life everlasting"? What is missing if we talk only about eternal life in heaven and not bodily resurrection?

Let students discuss openly without attempting to come to conclusions yet.

▪ I. THE FORGIVENESS OF SINS

Although "forgiveness of sins" is placed in the Third Article of the Creed, it's closely tied to each of the articles and to the work of each person of the Trinity. It is forgiveness—the removal of our sins, which lead to death—that makes possible everlasting life with God. (See Romans 6:23.)

A. The Father

God's nature as Father and Creator makes forgiveness both necessary and possible.

1. Regarding our need for forgiveness, read Malachi 1:6; Hosea 11:1–7; and Romans 1:18–23. What do we owe to God as our Father and Creator? Could you ever fully live this out?

Because God is our Father, we owe Him full honor and holy fear (Malachi 1:6), just as the Fourth Commandment calls us to honor our earthly father and mother—but even greater given that God is a perfect Father and the Father from whom every family is named (Ephesians 3:15). Hosea describes all of God's care for His people as the tender work of a Father: teaching His people to walk, healing, leading with love, bending down to feed. In response, we owe the Father love and obedience. Romans 1 teaches that in light of God's glory and power as Creator, we, His creatures, owe to Him honor and thanks.

None of us can ever live out the honor and obedience we owe to God. Like Israel in Hosea 11, we often give our fear, love, and trust to people and things other than God. We don't realize that it is He who has given us all things; instead we are bent on turning away. As Romans 1 describes, we have claimed our own wisdom rather than God's, dishonoring Him by our unrighteousness and idolatry.

2. Regarding God's mercy to forgive, read Isaiah 49:15–16; Isaiah 46:3–4; and Psalm 145:8–10. Why can we trust that we have forgiveness from the Father?

In Isaiah 49, in another tender parenting image, God compares Himself to a nursing mother. His love and faithfulness are greater even than that of a devoted earthly parent; despite our sins, God will not forget

His people. In Isaiah 46, God says that He who created us and bore us even before we were born is the same God who will carry and save us. From Psalm 145, we see that mercy, grace, and steadfast love are part of God's very character. God has mercy on His creation so that His people can give Him praise on earth.

B. The Son

God's mercy is given to us through the life, death, and resurrection of the Son.

Read Philippians 2:8; Matthew 3:16–17; and Romans 8:1–4, 14–17. How did Jesus fulfill the debt we owe to God, our Father and Creator? What does Romans 8 say about how Christ has taken away our sin and what this means for our relationship with God?

Jesus, the Son of God, was fully pleasing to His Father (Matthew 3:17), wholly obedient, even unto death (Philippians 2:8). He gave to God the honor, praise, and obedience that His fallen creatures never could. From Romans 8 we see that Christ took our sin upon Himself and gave us His righteousness in return. By faith in Christ, we are counted as having fulfilled all the requirements of the Law! We are free from condemnation and are made children of God and heirs of God's kingdom. When we are baptized into Christ, God says of us what He said of Jesus at His Baptism: "This is My beloved [child] with whom I am well pleased" (Matthew 3:17).

C. The Spirit

As the Small Catechism explains, we "receive this forgiveness through faith, that is, by believing the promise of the Gospel."[30] It is the work of the Spirit to give us such faith.

1. How do Romans 8:14–17 and Galatians 4:4–7 talk about the work of the Spirit?

The Spirit leads us, giving us faith to cry out to God as Father, and bearing witness that we are children of God. God sent His Son to redeem us; the Father and Son sent the Spirit, who gives us faith to call out to God as Father.

2. How and when do we receive this forgiveness of sins? Read Acts 2:38; Matthew 26:28; and John 20:22–23.

Through Baptism, God gives to us forgiveness of sins and the gift of the Holy Spirit. The Holy Spirit creates faith in us by which we can receive the gifts of the Gospel as won through the work of Jesus Christ. The Lord's Supper offers us forgiveness of sins received by faith and given through Jesus' body and blood sacrificed for us. The disciples were also told to speak forgiveness to others in Jesus' name. During confession and absolution (spoken in public worship or in private confession), we hear this forgiveness spoken aloud by our pastor, directly proclaimed as for you. We also as believers confess our sins to one another (James 5:16) and comfort one another with the truth of forgiveness freely given to us by faith in Jesus.

3. In what ways is it comforting to repeatedly see, taste, and hear our forgiveness in Word and Sacrament?

We know the forgiveness of sins was accomplished by Christ's death and resurrection and is freely and fully given to us by faith in Him. And yet, we may struggle to believe this is true when confronted with the graveness of our sin and its effects on others or when troubled by our ongoing struggle with sin. However, our confidence doesn't come because we feel forgiven or because of the strength of our faith. The Sacraments and the proclamation of forgiveness (both that spoken publicly and corporately and that spoken privately and in relationship with others) come from outside us, giving us visible and audible assurance of God's grace and mercy.

The forgiveness of sins powerfully impacts our lives here and now, as well as for eternity.

How does this forgiveness affect the following:

1. Our relationship with God? Read Hebrews 10:17–22.

Forgiveness is the only way in which we are able to approach the Father's throne, draw near to God, and have a relationship with Him.

2. Our relationships with others? Read Ephesians 4:31–32.

Only because we have been forgiven are we able to forgive others their sins against us. We have a new identity as forgiven children—we have put on the new self (Ephesians 4:24) —and this changes how we relate to others as both fellow sinners and fellow children for whom Christ died.

3. Our sanctified life (the Spirit's work to make us more like Christ)? Read Hebrews 10:14.

By Christ's sacrifice for the forgiveness of our sins, we have been made perfectly righteous in God's sight. This perfect and complete justification ("has perfected for all time") is what makes possible the Spirit's ongoing work to make us holy, to transform our thoughts, words, and actions to be more like Christ ("being sanctified").

II. WHY DOES THE RESURRECTION MATTER?

> But if there is no resurrection of the dead, then not even Christ has been raised. And if Christ has not

**been raised, then our preaching is in vain and your
faith is in vain.** (1 CORINTHIANS 15:13–14)

This is what the whole Apostles' Creed has been building to.

A. The First Article—God is our Father and Creator.

We were created to live forever in relationship with God. Read
Genesis 2:16–17 and Romans 6:23. Why did death enter the world?
Death came because of ..sin....

*B. The Second Article—Jesus lived, died, and rose for us.
Read John 10:10. Why did Jesus come?*

He came to bring ..life.to.the.full...

*C. The Third Article—the Holy Spirit works faith in Christ,
which grants forgiveness. Read Ephesians 1:13–14. What is
the relationship between the Spirit and eternal life?*

In Baptism, we have been sealed with the Holy Spirit. The Spirit
gives us faith in Christ, which grants forgiveness and eternal
life. This verse calls the Spirit a "guarantee" or "down payment"
on our eternal inheritance—the first fruits of God's gifts to us
which will be fully given in the new creation.

THE STORY OF THE BIBLE

*We were created for life with God. Sin separated us from
God and brought suffering and death. Jesus came to reconcile the world to God and give eternal, resurrected life.*

DIGGING DEEPER

Why is it that most people fight against death or fear it? When someone we love dies, why do we feel pain and sadness, anger and denial? Why do most cultures believe in some kind of life after death?

Could it be that death, as we know it, is not natural?

Discuss together. This is a difficult topic that may bring up painful feelings and memories for people. Don't push participants to feel one way, but certainly leave space for Christians to express hurt and anger about death. Jesus cried at Lazarus's tomb, even when He knew He was about to raise him. It is okay for Christians to mourn. Death frequently involves painful suffering, and it separates us from one another for a time.

Conclusion: Yes, death is unnatural. It is not part of God's original creation; it is the result of sin (Romans 5:12; 1 Corinthians 15:21–22). Death is an enemy to be disarmed and destroyed by Jesus (1 Corinthians 15:26, 55). Death is only "natural" because sin makes us and all living earthly creatures subject to death; it is all we have ever known in our life on earth.

III. THE RESURRECTION OF THE DEAD

A. Read John 5:28–29. Who will rise again?

All the dead will rise, believers and unbelievers alike.

B. Keep looking at John 5:28–29 and read Hebrews 9:27–28. What will be different for believers and unbelievers at the resurrection?

Believers will rise to life and salvation; unbelievers will rise to condemnation and hell. Every person faces judgment after death, but for believers, Jesus comes to save us from judgment and deliver us to everlasting life.

C. Read Job 19:25–27. Some people argue that resurrection is only spiritual. Other people believe in reincarnation. How does what Job says contradict both these ideas?

Job says he will see God in his flesh. We will have bodies in the resurrection. They will be a perfected version of us; we won't be reincarnated as someone or something else. In the same way, Elijah appeared with Jesus in his physical body at the transfiguration (Matthew 17:1–13), and Jesus, when He appeared to His disciples after the resurrection, had a physical body (see John 20:20; Luke 24:37–43), eating fish in front of them, and telling Thomas to touch His hands and His side.

IV. THE LIFE EVERLASTING

A. Read John 17:3 and John 3:36. How do believers have everlasting life right now?

Knowing God by faith in Jesus **is** everlasting life. Just as Adam and Eve suffered death when they sinned (not a future death but an immediate spiritual death as a consequence of their sin), eternal life begins now for us who believe in Jesus.

B. Read Ecclesiastes 12:7 and Luke 23:39–43. What happens as soon as a believer dies?

As soon as we die, our spirit is with God in eternal life. Jesus calls death only "sleep" (Mark 5:39–42; John 11:11); so, too, 1 Thessalonians 4:14

speaks of those who have died as having fallen asleep. What a beautiful, peaceful picture of what death is for the believer!

C. Read 1 Corinthians 15:21–23, 42–44, and 51–53. What will happen when Jesus comes back at the end of the world?

At the end, our bodies will be raised, perfect and imperishable.

DIGGING DEEPER

Resurrection is almost too incredible to believe. Everything we see on earth ends in death. What proof do we have that there is life after death?

We have evidence from Jesus' life that He has power to raise the dead (see the raising of Lazarus in John 11; Jairus's daughter in Mark 5:21–24, 25–43; and the widow's son in Luke 7:11–15).

In fact, the Bible is full of resurrection accounts. Consider two Old Testament accounts of the dead being raised: Elijah raising a widow's son (1 Kings 17:17–24) and Elisha raising a Shunammite's son (2 Kings 4:18–37). Even after Elisha's death, a man was restored to life when his body was thrown atop Elisha's bones in his grave (2 Kings 13:21). Another lesser known New Testament resurrection account is that of the saints who rose with Jesus on Easter (Matthew 27:52–53). Also both Peter (Acts 9:36–42) and Paul (Acts 20:7–10) raised people from the dead by Christ's power.

Clearly, Jesus is stronger than death. However, each of these resurrections was just a foretaste of the true, final resurrection—a small glimpse of the final glory spilling out through Jesus, the prophets, and the apostles. Each of the people raised in biblical accounts at some point died again. But Christ was raised in glory, never to die again (Romans 6:9). Our solid proof, the only proof we need, is Jesus' own resurrection from the dead! See 1 Corinthians 15:3–8 (Jesus' post-resurrection appearances) and 1 Corinthians 15:20–23 (Christ's resurrection is the promise of our own resurrection).

D. What will this eternal life be like?

John's description of eternal life brings much hope and joy:

> **And I heard a loud voice from the throne saying, "Behold, the dwelling place of God is with man. He will dwell with them, and they will be His people, and God Himself will be with them as their God. He will wipe away every tear from their eyes, and death shall be no more, neither shall there be mourning, nor crying, nor pain anymore, for the former things have passed away."** (REVELATION 21:3–4)

E. What will be the best part of eternal life?

We will be with God. Any other answer is missing the point of our faith. The end of sadness, dying, pain, and such—even being reunited with loved ones—is just wonderful icing on the cake!

▪ PRAYER PROMPTS

- *Praise God for the gift of eternal life, now and in heaven.*
- *Pray for those who are sick and dying and those who love and care for them. Pray for the echo of Jesus' empty tomb to ring out loudly in their hearts.*
- *Pray for grace to live each day in light of eternity.*

▐ CLOSING

Sing the hymn on page 108 together.

As time allows, review the essay "But We'll See Jesus" on page 110, or encourage participants to read the essay on their own outside of class.

ENDNOTES

■ ■ ■

1   *LSB*, "For grace to receive the Word," p. 308.

2   Large Catechism, Part 2, paragraph 1.

3   Small Catechism, explanation of the First Commandment.

4   Large Catechism, Part 2, Second Article, paragraph 33.

5   Large Catechism, Part 2, Third Article, paragraph 58.

6   Small Catechism, First Article.

7   Questions adapted from Jim Found, "Eight Bible Topics for New Christians: Lesson 2—What Is God Like?" Accessed January 16, 2022, https://foundbytes.com/eight2/.

8   Small Catechism, Second Commandment.

9   *Small Catechism*, Second Article.

10 Questions about John 3:16 adapted from Jim Found, "Eight Bible Topics for New Christians: Lesson 3—Knowing Jesus through His Names." Accessed January 16, 2022, https://foundbytes.com/eight3/.

11 Statements ibid.

12 Small Catechism, The Sacrament of Holy Baptism, "The Blessings of Baptism," Second.

13 Small Catechism, Third Article.

14 Small Catechism, Questions and Answers, Apostles' Creed, II. The Church, the Communion of Saints.

15 Small Catechism, Questions and Answers, Apostles' Creed, IV. The Resurrection of the Body V. The Life Everlasting.

16 Small Catechism, Question 184.

17 *LSB*, "For grace to receive the Word," p. 308.

18 Small Catechism, First Article.

19 Questions adapted from Jim Found, "Eight Bible Topics for New Christians: Lesson 2—What Is God Like?" Accessed January 16, 2022, https://foundbytes.com/eight2/.

20 Small Catechism, Second Commandment.

21 Small Catechism, Second Article.

22 Questions about John 3:16 adapted from: Jim Found, "Eight Bible Topics for New Christians: Lesson 3—Knowing Jesus through His Names." Accessed January 16, 2022, https://foundbytes.com/eight3/.

23 Statements adapted from: Jim Found, "Eight Bible Topics for New Christians: Lesson 3—Knowing Jesus through His Names." Accessed January 16, 2022, https://foundbytes.com/eight3/.

24   Small Catechism, Third Article.

25   Small Catechism, Baptism, "The Power of Baptism," Third.

26   *Luther's Works*, American Edition, volume 21, page 229

27   If more questions on Baptism arise, see the explanation of Baptism in *Luther's Small Catechism with Explanation*, Questions 297–342.

28   Small Catechism, Questions and Answers, Apostles' Creed, II. The Church, the Communion of Saints.

29   Small Catechism, Questions and Answers, Apostles' Creed, IV. The Resurrection of the Body V. The Life Everlasting.

30   Small Catechism, Question 184.